Integrated Architecture Framework
Complete Self-Assessment Guide

The guidance in this Self-Assessment is based on Integrated Archite̶
Framework best practices and standards in business process architecture,
design and quality management. The guidance is also based on the
professional judgment of the individual collaborators listed in the
Acknowledgments.

Table of Contents

About The Art of Service

The Art of Service, Business Process Architects since 2000, is dedicated to helping stakeholders achieve excellence.

Defining, designing, creating, and implementing a process to solve a stakeholders challenge or meet an objective is the most valuable role… In EVERY group, company, organization and department.

Unless you're talking a one-time, single-use project, there should be a process. Whether that process is managed and implemented by humans, AI, or a combination of the two, it needs to be designed by someone with a complex enough perspective to ask the right questions.

Someone capable of asking the right questions and step back and say, 'What are we really trying to accomplish here? And is there a different way to look at it?'

With The Art of Service's Standard Requirements Self-Assessments, we empower people who can do just that — whether their title is marketer, entrepreneur, manager, salesperson, consultant, Business Process Manager, executive assistant, IT Manager, CIO etc... —they are the people who rule the future. They are people who watch the process as it happens, and ask the right questions to make the process work better.

Contact us when you need any support with this Self-Assessment and any help with templates, blue-prints and examples of standard documents you might need:

http://theartofservice.com
service@theartofservice.com

Included Resources - how to access

Included with your purchase of the book is the Integrated

Architecture Framework Self-Assessment Spreadsheet Dashboard which contains all questions and Self-Assessment areas and auto-generates insights, graphs, and project RACI planning - all with examples to get you started right away.

How? Simply send an email to
access@theartofservice.com
with this books' title in the subject to get the Integrated Architecture Framework Self Assessment Tool right away.

You will receive the following contents with New and Updated specific criteria:

- The latest quick edition of the book in PDF

- The latest complete edition of the book in PDF, which criteria correspond to the criteria in...

- The Self-Assessment Excel Dashboard, and...

- Example pre-filled Self-Assessment Excel Dashboard to get familiar with results generation

- In-depth specific Checklists covering the topic

- Project management checklists and templates to assist with implementation

INCLUDES LIFETIME SELF ASSESSMENT UPDATES

Every self assessment comes with Lifetime Updates and Lifetime Free Updated Books. Lifetime Updates is an industry-first feature which allows you to receive verified self assessment updates, ensuring you always have the most accurate information at your fingertips.

Get it now- you will be glad you did - do it now, before you forget.

Send an email to **access@theartofservice.com** with this books' title in the subject to get the Integrated Architecture Framework Self Assessment Tool right away.

Purpose of this Self-Assessment

This Self-Assessment has been developed to improve understanding of the requirements and elements of Integrated Architecture Framework, based on best practices and standards in business process architecture, design and quality management.

It is designed to allow for a rapid Self-Assessment to determine how closely existing management practices and procedures correspond to the elements of the Self-Assessment.

The criteria of requirements and elements of Integrated Architecture Framework have been rephrased in the format of a Self-Assessment questionnaire, with a seven-criterion scoring system, as explained in this document.

In this format, even with limited background knowledge of Integrated Architecture Framework, a manager can quickly review existing operations to determine how they measure up to the standards. This in turn can serve as the starting point of a 'gap analysis' to identify management tools or system elements that might usefully be implemented in the organization to help improve overall performance.

How to use the Self-Assessment

On the following pages are a series of questions to identify to what extent your Integrated Architecture Framework initiative is complete in comparison to the requirements set in standards.

To facilitate answering the questions, there is a space in front of each question to enter a score on a scale of '1' to '5'.

1 Strongly Disagree

2 Disagree

3 Neutral

4 Agree

5 Strongly Agree

Read the question and rate it with the following in front of mind:

'In my belief, the answer to this question is clearly defined'.

There are two ways in which you can choose to interpret this statement;
1. how aware are you that the answer to the question is clearly defined
2. for more in-depth analysis you can choose to gather evidence and confirm the answer to the question. This obviously will take more time, most Self-Assessment users opt for the first way to interpret the question and dig deeper later on based on the outcome of the overall Self-Assessment.

A score of '1' would mean that the answer is not clear at all, where a '5' would mean the answer is crystal clear and defined. Leave emtpy when the question is not applicable or you don't want to answer it, you can skip it without affecting your score. Write your score in the space provided.

After you have responded to all the appropriate statements in each section, compute your average score for that section, using the formula provided, and round to the nearest tenth. Then transfer to the corresponding spoke in the Integrated Architecture Framework Scorecard on the second next page of the Self-Assessment.

Your completed Integrated Architecture Framework Scorecard will give you a clear presentation of which Integrated Architecture Framework areas need attention.

Integrated Architecture Framework Scorecard Example

Example of how the finalized Scorecard can look like:

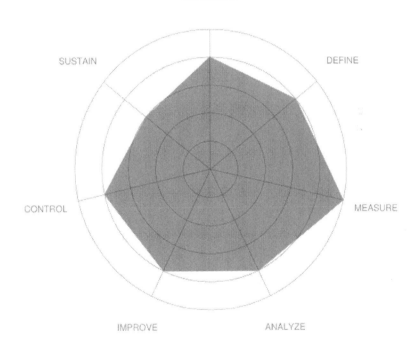

Integrated Architecture Framework Scorecard

Your Scores:

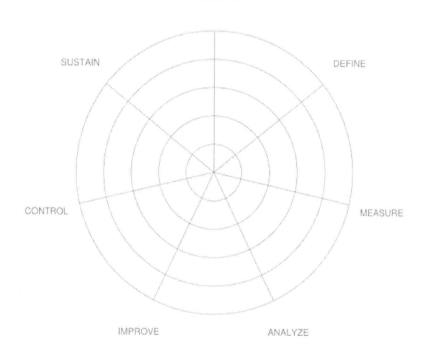

BEGINNING OF THE SELF-ASSESSMENT:

CRITERION #1: RECOGNIZE

INTENT: Be aware of the need for change. Recognize that there is an unfavorable variation, problem or symptom.

In my belief, the answer to this question is clearly defined:

5 Strongly Agree

4 Agree

3 Neutral

2 Disagree

1 Strongly Disagree

1. What needs to be done?
<--- Score

2. How do you identify the kinds of information that you will need?
<--- Score

3. As a sponsor, customer or management, how important is it to meet goals, objectives?

<--- Score

4. What are the timeframes required to resolve each of the issues/problems?
<--- Score

5. Do you need to avoid or amend any Integrated Architecture Framework activities?
<--- Score

6. What is the Integrated Architecture Framework problem definition? What do you need to resolve?
<--- Score

7. Why is this needed?
<--- Score

8. Who needs to know about Integrated Architecture Framework?
<--- Score

9. Who defines the rules in relation to any given issue?
<--- Score

10. What resources or support might you need?
<--- Score

11. How do you take a forward-looking perspective in identifying Integrated Architecture Framework research related to market response and models?
<--- Score

12. How do you recognize an objection?
<--- Score

13. Who needs budgets?

<--- Score

14. Is it clear when you think of the day ahead of you what activities and tasks you need to complete?

<--- Score

15. Who needs to know?

<--- Score

16. How does it fit into your organizational needs and tasks?

<--- Score

17. What is the problem or issue?

<--- Score

18. Are problem definition and motivation clearly presented?

<--- Score

19. What would happen if Integrated Architecture Framework weren't done?

<--- Score

20. What does Integrated Architecture Framework success mean to the stakeholders?

<--- Score

21. What vendors make products that address the Integrated Architecture Framework needs?

<--- Score

22. Are there Integrated Architecture Framework problems defined?

<--- Score

23. What is the smallest subset of the problem you can usefully solve?
<--- Score

24. Who should resolve the Integrated Architecture Framework issues?
<--- Score

25. What information do users need?
<--- Score

26. Will Integrated Architecture Framework deliverables need to be tested and, if so, by whom?
<--- Score

27. Can management personnel recognize the monetary benefit of Integrated Architecture Framework?
<--- Score

28. Are there any revenue recognition issues?
<--- Score

29. How do you recognize an Integrated Architecture Framework objection?
<--- Score

30. What should be considered when identifying available resources, constraints, and deadlines?
<--- Score

31. Are your goals realistic? Do you need to redefine your problem? Perhaps the problem has changed or maybe you have reached your goal

and need to set a new one?
<--- Score

32. How do you assess your Integrated Architecture Framework workforce capability and capacity needs, including skills, competencies, and staffing levels?
<--- Score

33. For your Integrated Architecture Framework project, identify and describe the business environment, is there more than one layer to the business environment?
<--- Score

34. What problems are you facing and how do you consider Integrated Architecture Framework will circumvent those obstacles?
<--- Score

35. Is it needed?
<--- Score

36. What prevents you from making the changes you know will make you a more effective Integrated Architecture Framework leader?
<--- Score

37. What is the recognized need?
<--- Score

38. Is the quality assurance team identified?
<--- Score

39. Are controls defined to recognize and contain problems?
<--- Score

40. Which issues are too important to ignore?
<--- Score

41. What do you need to start doing?
<--- Score

42. To what extent does each concerned units management team recognize Integrated Architecture Framework as an effective investment?
<--- Score

43. Who are your key stakeholders who need to sign off?
<--- Score

44. How much are sponsors, customers, partners, stakeholders involved in Integrated Architecture Framework? In other words, what are the risks, if Integrated Architecture Framework does not deliver successfully?
<--- Score

45. What activities does the governance board need to consider?
<--- Score

46. How are you going to measure success?
<--- Score

47. What tools and technologies are needed for a custom Integrated Architecture Framework project?
<--- Score

48. Are you dealing with any of the same issues today as yesterday? What can you do about this?

<--- Score

49. Whom do you really need or want to serve?
<--- Score

50. Do you know what you need to know about Integrated Architecture Framework?
<--- Score

51. What is the problem and/or vulnerability?
<--- Score

52. Does Integrated Architecture Framework create potential expectations in other areas that need to be recognized and considered?
<--- Score

53. How can auditing be a preventative security measure?
<--- Score

54. Are there recognized Integrated Architecture Framework problems?
<--- Score

55. How are training requirements identified?
<--- Score

56. What situation(s) led to this Integrated Architecture Framework Self Assessment?
<--- Score

57. Who else hopes to benefit from it?
<--- Score

58. Where do you need to exercise leadership?

<--- Score

59. What Integrated Architecture Framework problem should be solved?
<--- Score

60. Looking at each person individually – does every one have the qualities which are needed to work in this group?
<--- Score

61. Are losses recognized in a timely manner?
<--- Score

62. Think about the people you identified for your Integrated Architecture Framework project and the project responsibilities you would assign to them, what kind of training do you think they would need to perform these responsibilities effectively?
<--- Score

63. What is the extent or complexity of the Integrated Architecture Framework problem?
<--- Score

64. When a Integrated Architecture Framework manager recognizes a problem, what options are available?
<--- Score

65. Does your organization need more Integrated Architecture Framework education?
<--- Score

66. Which needs are not included or involved?
<--- Score

67. What Integrated Architecture Framework capabilities do you need?

<--- Score

68. What are the Integrated Architecture Framework resources needed?

<--- Score

69. Are employees recognized for desired behaviors?

<--- Score

70. Why the need?

<--- Score

71. What are the minority interests and what amount of minority interests can be recognized?

<--- Score

72. What needs to stay?

<--- Score

73. Who needs what information?

<--- Score

74. What Integrated Architecture Framework events should you attend?

<--- Score

75. Is the need for organizational change recognized?

<--- Score

76. What are the expected benefits of Integrated Architecture Framework to the stakeholder?

<--- Score

77. Do you need different information or graphics?
<--- Score

78. How do you identify subcontractor relationships?
<--- Score

79. Will new equipment/products be required to facilitate Integrated Architecture Framework delivery, for example is new software needed?
<--- Score

80. To what extent would your organization benefit from being recognized as a award recipient?
<--- Score

81. What extra resources will you need?
<--- Score

82. Are employees recognized or rewarded for performance that demonstrates the highest levels of integrity?
<--- Score

83. What creative shifts do you need to take?
<--- Score

84. What are the clients issues and concerns?
<--- Score

85. Have you identified your Integrated Architecture Framework key performance indicators?
<--- Score

86. Do you recognize Integrated Architecture Framework achievements?

<--- Score

87. Would you recognize a threat from the inside?
<--- Score

88. Which information does the Integrated Architecture Framework business case need to include?
<--- Score

89. Are there any specific expectations or concerns about the Integrated Architecture Framework team, Integrated Architecture Framework itself?
<--- Score

90. Does the problem have ethical dimensions?
<--- Score

91. Will a response program recognize when a crisis occurs and provide some level of response?
<--- Score

92. What else needs to be measured?
<--- Score

93. What training and capacity building actions are needed to implement proposed reforms?
<--- Score

94. How are the Integrated Architecture Framework's objectives aligned to the group's overall stakeholder strategy?
<--- Score

95. Consider your own Integrated Architecture Framework project, what types of organizational

problems do you think might be causing or affecting your problem, based on the work done so far?
<--- Score

96. What Integrated Architecture Framework coordination do you need?
<--- Score

97. Will it solve real problems?
<--- Score

98. What are the stakeholder objectives to be achieved with Integrated Architecture Framework?
<--- Score

99. Did you miss any major Integrated Architecture Framework issues?
<--- Score

Add up total points for this section:
_ _ _ _ _ = Total points for this section

Divided by: _ _ _ _ _ _ (number of statements answered) = _ _ _ _ _ _
Average score for this section

Transfer your score to the Integrated Architecture Framework Index at the beginning of the Self-Assessment.

CRITERION #2: DEFINE:

INTENT: Formulate the stakeholder problem. Define the problem, needs and objectives.

In my belief, the answer to this question is clearly defined:

5 Strongly Agree

4 Agree

3 Neutral

2 Disagree

1 Strongly Disagree

1. What are the boundaries of the scope? What is in bounds and what is not? What is the start point? What is the stop point?
<--- Score

2. What information do you gather?
<--- Score

3. When is/was the Integrated Architecture

Framework start date?
<--- Score

4. Is there a critical path to deliver Integrated Architecture Framework results?
<--- Score

5. How will variation in the actual durations of each activity be dealt with to ensure that the expected Integrated Architecture Framework results are met?
<--- Score

6. What scope to assess?
<--- Score

7. What scope do you want your strategy to cover?
<--- Score

8. Is Integrated Architecture Framework linked to key stakeholder goals and objectives?
<--- Score

9. How often are the team meetings?
<--- Score

10. What is the scope?
<--- Score

11. Do you have a Integrated Architecture Framework success story or case study ready to tell and share?
<--- Score

12. Is data collected and displayed to better understand customer(s) critical needs and requirements.
<--- Score

13. How can the value of Integrated Architecture Framework be defined?
<--- Score

14. What would be the goal or target for a Integrated Architecture Framework's improvement team?
<--- Score

15. What are the dynamics of the communication plan?
<--- Score

16. How do you manage unclear Integrated Architecture Framework requirements?
<--- Score

17. Is there a clear Integrated Architecture Framework case definition?
<--- Score

18. Have specific policy objectives been defined?
<--- Score

19. Has your scope been defined?
<--- Score

20. Are audit criteria, scope, frequency and methods defined?
<--- Score

21. Does the scope remain the same?
<--- Score

22. What are the Roles and Responsibilities for each team member and its leadership? Where is this

documented?

<--- Score

23. How do you think the partners involved in Integrated Architecture Framework would have defined success?

<--- Score

24. What is in the scope and what is not in scope?

<--- Score

25. Is there any additional Integrated Architecture Framework definition of success?

<--- Score

26. Scope of sensitive information?

<--- Score

27. Have all basic functions of Integrated Architecture Framework been defined?

<--- Score

28. What Integrated Architecture Framework requirements should be gathered?

<--- Score

29. Are roles and responsibilities formally defined?

<--- Score

30. How do you gather requirements?

<--- Score

31. Is there a completed, verified, and validated high-level 'as is' (not 'should be' or 'could be') stakeholder process map?

<--- Score

32. Do you have organizational privacy requirements?

<--- Score

33. In what way can you redefine the criteria of choice clients have in your category in your favor?

<--- Score

34. Are accountability and ownership for Integrated Architecture Framework clearly defined?

<--- Score

35. How do you hand over Integrated Architecture Framework context?

<--- Score

36. Where can you gather more information?

<--- Score

37. Are different versions of process maps needed to account for the different types of inputs?

<--- Score

38. Has the improvement team collected the 'voice of the customer' (obtained feedback – qualitative and quantitative)?

<--- Score

39. Is special Integrated Architecture Framework user knowledge required?

<--- Score

40. How do you manage scope?

<--- Score

41. Has a Integrated Architecture Framework requirement not been met?
<--- Score

42. Do you all define Integrated Architecture Framework in the same way?
<--- Score

43. What is the scope of Integrated Architecture Framework?
<--- Score

44. The political context: who holds power?
<--- Score

45. Are task requirements clearly defined?
<--- Score

46. How would you define Integrated Architecture Framework leadership?
<--- Score

47. When are meeting minutes sent out? Who is on the distribution list?
<--- Score

48. Has a high-level 'as is' process map been completed, verified and validated?
<--- Score

49. What is in scope?
<--- Score

50. Are approval levels defined for contracts and supplements to contracts?
<--- Score

51. Is there a Integrated Architecture Framework management charter, including stakeholder case, problem and goal statements, scope, milestones, roles and responsibilities, communication plan?
<--- Score

52. What constraints exist that might impact the team?
<--- Score

53. What Integrated Architecture Framework services do you require?
<--- Score

54. Who are the Integrated Architecture Framework improvement team members, including Management Leads and Coaches?
<--- Score

55. How did the Integrated Architecture Framework manager receive input to the development of a Integrated Architecture Framework improvement plan and the estimated completion dates/times of each activity?
<--- Score

56. Why are you doing Integrated Architecture Framework and what is the scope?
<--- Score

57. What customer feedback methods were used to solicit their input?
<--- Score

58. When is the estimated completion date?

<--- Score

59. Are resources adequate for the scope?
<--- Score

60. Has everyone on the team, including the team leaders, been properly trained?
<--- Score

61. Is Integrated Architecture Framework currently on schedule according to the plan?
<--- Score

62. What are the Integrated Architecture Framework tasks and definitions?
<--- Score

63. Is it clearly defined in and to your organization what you do?
<--- Score

64. What is the context?
<--- Score

65. Are required metrics defined, what are they?
<--- Score

66. How would you define the culture at your organization, how susceptible is it to Integrated Architecture Framework changes?
<--- Score

67. What are the compelling stakeholder reasons for embarking on Integrated Architecture Framework?
<--- Score

68. How do you build the right business case?

<--- Score

69. What is the worst case scenario?

<--- Score

70. What is the scope of the Integrated Architecture Framework work?

<--- Score

71. What was the context?

<--- Score

72. How have you defined all Integrated Architecture Framework requirements first?

<--- Score

73. What critical content must be communicated – who, what, when, where, and how?

<--- Score

74. How will the Integrated Architecture Framework team and the group measure complete success of Integrated Architecture Framework?

<--- Score

75. What baselines are required to be defined and managed?

<--- Score

76. What are the tasks and definitions?

<--- Score

77. Does the team have regular meetings?

<--- Score

78. Has the direction changed at all during the course of Integrated Architecture Framework? If so, when did it change and why?
<--- Score

79. Have the customer needs been translated into specific, measurable requirements? How?
<--- Score

80. Has a project plan, Gantt chart, or similar been developed/completed?
<--- Score

81. Are all requirements met?
<--- Score

82. How do you gather the stories?
<--- Score

83. Has the Integrated Architecture Framework work been fairly and/or equitably divided and delegated among team members who are qualified and capable to perform the work? Has everyone contributed?
<--- Score

84. Is the team adequately staffed with the desired cross-functionality? If not, what additional resources are available to the team?
<--- Score

85. Has anyone else (internal or external to the group) attempted to solve this problem or a similar one before? If so, what knowledge can be leveraged from these previous efforts?
<--- Score

86. What are the requirements for audit information?
<--- Score

87. Who defines (or who defined) the rules and roles?
<--- Score

88. What are the record-keeping requirements of Integrated Architecture Framework activities?
<--- Score

89. What system do you use for gathering Integrated Architecture Framework information?
<--- Score

90. What are the Integrated Architecture Framework use cases?
<--- Score

91. Are there different segments of customers?
<--- Score

92. What key stakeholder process output measure(s) does Integrated Architecture Framework leverage and how?
<--- Score

93. What sources do you use to gather information for a Integrated Architecture Framework study?
<--- Score

94. How do you gather Integrated Architecture Framework requirements?
<--- Score

95. What is a worst-case scenario for losses?

<--- Score

96. Is Integrated Architecture Framework required?
<--- Score

97. What specifically is the problem? Where does it occur? When does it occur? What is its extent?
<--- Score

98. Who is gathering Integrated Architecture Framework information?
<--- Score

99. Are the Integrated Architecture Framework requirements testable?
<--- Score

100. Who is gathering information?
<--- Score

101. Are there any constraints known that bear on the ability to perform Integrated Architecture Framework work? How is the team addressing them?
<--- Score

102. Are the Integrated Architecture Framework requirements complete?
<--- Score

103. What sort of initial information to gather?
<--- Score

104. What are (control) requirements for Integrated Architecture Framework Information?
<--- Score

105. Is the work to date meeting requirements?
<--- Score

106. Is the Integrated Architecture Framework scope manageable?
<--- Score

107. What is the scope of the Integrated Architecture Framework effort?
<--- Score

108. How was the 'as is' process map developed, reviewed, verified and validated?
<--- Score

109. Has/have the customer(s) been identified?
<--- Score

110. How are consistent Integrated Architecture Framework definitions important?
<--- Score

111. How does the Integrated Architecture Framework manager ensure against scope creep?
<--- Score

112. What is out-of-scope initially?
<--- Score

113. Is there regularly 100% attendance at the team meetings? If not, have appointed substitutes attended to preserve cross-functionality and full representation?
<--- Score

114. What is the definition of Integrated Architecture Framework excellence?
<--- Score

115. What are the core elements of the Integrated Architecture Framework business case?
<--- Score

116. Will a Integrated Architecture Framework production readiness review be required?
<--- Score

117. Is there a completed SIPOC representation, describing the Suppliers, Inputs, Process, Outputs, and Customers?
<--- Score

118. How do you manage changes in Integrated Architecture Framework requirements?
<--- Score

119. What intelligence can you gather?
<--- Score

120. Do the problem and goal statements meet the SMART criteria (specific, measurable, attainable, relevant, and time-bound)?
<--- Score

121. What is out of scope?
<--- Score

122. Has a team charter been developed and communicated?
<--- Score

123. If substitutes have been appointed, have they been briefed on the Integrated Architecture Framework goals and received regular communications as to the progress to date?
<--- Score

124. What are the rough order estimates on cost savings/opportunities that Integrated Architecture Framework brings?
<--- Score

125. How is the team tracking and documenting its work?
<--- Score

126. Who approved the Integrated Architecture Framework scope?
<--- Score

127. How and when will the baselines be defined?
<--- Score

128. What knowledge or experience is required?
<--- Score

129. Is the current 'as is' process being followed? If not, what are the discrepancies?
<--- Score

130. How do you keep key subject matter experts in the loop?
<--- Score

131. Is the improvement team aware of the different versions of a process: what they think it is vs. what it actually is vs. what it should be vs. what it could be?

<--- Score

Add up total points for this section:
_____ = Total points for this section

Divided by: _____ (number of
statements answered) = _____
Average score for this section

Transfer your score to the Integrated
Architecture Framework Index at the
beginning of the Self-Assessment.

CRITERION #3: MEASURE:

In my belief, the answer to this
question is clearly defined:

5 Strongly Agree

4 Agree

3 Neutral

2 Disagree

1 Strongly Disagree

1. What are the current costs of the Integrated
Architecture Framework process?
<--- Score

2. When are costs are incurred?
<--- Score

3. What users will be impacted?
<--- Score

4. How do you verify your resources?
<--- Score

5. What do you measure and why?
<--- Score

6. Are there measurements based on task performance?
<--- Score

7. What is an unallowable cost?
<--- Score

8. How do you measure variability?
<--- Score

9. How sensitive must the Integrated Architecture Framework strategy be to cost?
<--- Score

10. What does your operating model cost?
<--- Score

11. What details are required of the Integrated Architecture Framework cost structure?
<--- Score

12. How do you measure success?
<--- Score

13. How is performance measured?
<--- Score

14. What causes extra work or rework?
<--- Score

15. What are the Integrated Architecture Framework investment costs?

<--- Score

16. Which costs should be taken into account?

<--- Score

17. What are the types and number of measures to use?

<--- Score

18. Are supply costs steady or fluctuating?

<--- Score

19. Was a business case (cost/benefit) developed?

<--- Score

20. What are the Integrated Architecture Framework key cost drivers?

<--- Score

21. How can you manage cost down?

<--- Score

22. How will success or failure be measured?

<--- Score

23. Are missed Integrated Architecture Framework opportunities costing your organization money?

<--- Score

24. What drives O&M cost?

<--- Score

25. How do you measure efficient delivery of

Integrated Architecture Framework services?
<--- Score

26. Has a cost center been established?
<--- Score

27. At what cost?
<--- Score

28. How do your measurements capture actionable
Integrated Architecture Framework information for
use in exceeding your customers expectations and
securing your customers engagement?
<--- Score

29. What would it cost to replace your technology?
<--- Score

30. Where is it measured?
<--- Score

31. How do you measure lifecycle phases?
<--- Score

32. What does losing customers cost your
organization?
<--- Score

**33. What is the total cost related to deploying
Integrated Architecture Framework, including any
consulting or professional services?**
<--- Score

34. Do you have an issue in getting priority?
<--- Score

35. Do you have a flow diagram of what happens?
<--- Score

36. Will Integrated Architecture Framework have
an impact on current business continuity, disaster
recovery processes and/or infrastructure?
<--- Score

37. What are hidden Integrated Architecture
Framework quality costs?
<--- Score

38. What causes investor action?
<--- Score

39. What potential environmental factors impact the
Integrated Architecture Framework effort?
<--- Score

40. How do you verify and develop ideas and
innovations?
<--- Score

41. What do people want to verify?
<--- Score

42. What is your Integrated Architecture Framework
quality cost segregation study?
<--- Score

43. What are your key Integrated Architecture
Framework organizational performance measures,
including key short and longer-term financial
measures?
<--- Score

44. Did you tackle the cause or the symptom?
<--- Score

45. Where can you go to verify the info?
<--- Score

46. What are your primary costs, revenues, assets?
<--- Score

47. Are indirect costs charged to the Integrated Architecture Framework program?
<--- Score

48. How can a Integrated Architecture Framework test verify your ideas or assumptions?
<--- Score

49. What is the root cause(s) of the problem?
<--- Score

50. What are the costs and benefits?
<--- Score

51. What tests verify requirements?
<--- Score

52. Is the cost worth the Integrated Architecture Framework effort ?
<--- Score

53. Are Integrated Architecture Framework vulnerabilities categorized and prioritized?
<--- Score

54. Among the Integrated Architecture Framework product and service cost to be estimated, which is

considered hardest to estimate?
<--- Score

55. Are the units of measure consistent?
<--- Score

56. How will measures be used to manage and adapt?
<--- Score

57. Do you have any cost Integrated Architecture Framework limitation requirements?
<--- Score

58. How do you verify if Integrated Architecture Framework is built right?
<--- Score

59. What does a Test Case verify?
<--- Score

60. Is there an opportunity to verify requirements?
<--- Score

61. Do you effectively measure and reward individual and team performance?
<--- Score

62. Are there competing Integrated Architecture Framework priorities?
<--- Score

63. What harm might be caused?
<--- Score

64. How do you quantify and qualify impacts?
<--- Score

65. Are you able to realize any cost savings?
<--- Score

66. Why do you expend time and effort to implement measurement, for whom?
<--- Score

67. How are costs allocated?
<--- Score

68. What are the costs?
<--- Score

69. Have design-to-cost goals been established?
<--- Score

70. When should you bother with diagrams?
<--- Score

71. What disadvantage does this cause for the user?
<--- Score

72. What is measured? Why?
<--- Score

73. What are your customers expectations and measures?
<--- Score

74. What are the strategic priorities for this year?
<--- Score

75. How do you verify the authenticity of the data and information used?

<--- Score

76. How do you prevent mis-estimating cost?
<--- Score

77. What are you verifying?
<--- Score

78. How do you verify performance?
<--- Score

79. What is your decision requirements diagram?
<--- Score

80. What measurements are being captured?
<--- Score

81. How is progress measured?
<--- Score

82. How long to keep data and how to manage retention costs?
<--- Score

83. Have you made assumptions about the shape of the future, particularly its impact on your customers and competitors?
<--- Score

84. Which Integrated Architecture Framework impacts are significant?
<--- Score

85. How can you measure the performance?
<--- Score

86. Where is the cost?
<--- Score

87. How will costs be allocated?
<--- Score

88. How will your organization measure success?
<--- Score

89. How much does it cost?
<--- Score

90. What are the costs of delaying Integrated Architecture Framework action?
<--- Score

91. What are your operating costs?
<--- Score

92. Are you aware of what could cause a problem?
<--- Score

93. Is it possible to estimate the impact of unanticipated complexity such as wrong or failed assumptions, feedback, etcetera on proposed reforms?
<--- Score

94. Are you taking your company in the direction of better and revenue or cheaper and cost?
<--- Score

95. Why do the measurements/indicators matter?
<--- Score

96. What would be a real cause for concern?

<--- Score

97. Who pays the cost?
<--- Score

98. What methods are feasible and acceptable to estimate the impact of reforms?
<--- Score

99. How to cause the change?
<--- Score

100. How will you measure your Integrated Architecture Framework effectiveness?
<--- Score

101. How do you verify the Integrated Architecture Framework requirements quality?
<--- Score

102. Who should receive measurement reports?
<--- Score

103. How will effects be measured?
<--- Score

104. Are there any easy-to-implement alternatives to Integrated Architecture Framework? Sometimes other solutions are available that do not require the cost implications of a full-blown project?
<--- Score

105. How are measurements made?
<--- Score

106. Are the Integrated Architecture Framework

benefits worth its costs?
<--- Score

107. Does a Integrated Architecture Framework quantification method exist?
<--- Score

108. What measurements are possible, practicable and meaningful?
<--- Score

109. Is the solution cost-effective?
<--- Score

110. How can you reduce costs?
<--- Score

111. Do the benefits outweigh the costs?
<--- Score

112. How can you reduce the costs of obtaining inputs?
<--- Score

113. Does the Integrated Architecture Framework task fit the client's priorities?
<--- Score

114. What are allowable costs?
<--- Score

115. What are the operational costs after Integrated Architecture Framework deployment?
<--- Score

116. What evidence is there and what is measured?

<--- Score

117. How can you measure Integrated Architecture Framework in a systematic way?
<--- Score

118. Do you aggressively reward and promote the people who have the biggest impact on creating excellent Integrated Architecture Framework services/products?
<--- Score

119. What causes mismanagement?
<--- Score

120. What is the cost of rework?
<--- Score

121. What are the estimated costs of proposed changes?
<--- Score

122. What are the costs of reform?
<--- Score

123. Which measures and indicators matter?
<--- Score

124. How do you verify and validate the Integrated Architecture Framework data?
<--- Score

125. How is the value delivered by Integrated Architecture Framework being measured?
<--- Score

126. Are the measurements objective?
<--- Score

127. When a disaster occurs, who gets priority?
<--- Score

128. What is the cause of any Integrated Architecture Framework gaps?
<--- Score

129. Have you included everything in your Integrated Architecture Framework cost models?
<--- Score

130. How do you control the overall costs of your work processes?
<--- Score

131. What causes innovation to fail or succeed in your organization?
<--- Score

Add up total points for this section:
_____ = Total points for this section

Divided by: _____ (number of statements answered) = _____
Average score for this section

Transfer your score to the Integrated Architecture Framework Index at the beginning of the Self-Assessment.

CRITERION #4: ANALYZE:

INTENT: Analyze causes, assumptions
and hypotheses.

In my belief, the answer to this
question is clearly defined:

5 Strongly Agree

4 Agree

3 Neutral

2 Disagree

1 Strongly Disagree

1. What is your organizations system for selecting qualified vendors?
<--- Score

2. What are the Integrated Architecture Framework business drivers?
<--- Score

3. How does the organization define, manage, and improve its Integrated Architecture Framework

processes?
<--- Score

4. Should you invest in industry-recognized qualifications?
<--- Score

5. What conclusions were drawn from the team's data collection and analysis? How did the team reach these conclusions?
<--- Score

6. An organizationally feasible system request is one that considers the mission, goals and objectives of the organization, key questions are: is the Integrated Architecture Framework solution request practical and will it solve a problem or take advantage of an opportunity to achieve company goals?
<--- Score

7. Is the required Integrated Architecture Framework data gathered?
<--- Score

8. What is the Value Stream Mapping?
<--- Score

9. What internal processes need improvement?
<--- Score

10. How is the way you as the leader think and process information affecting your organizational culture?
<--- Score

11. Do several people in different organizational units assist with the Integrated Architecture

Framework process?
<--- Score

12. Is data and process analysis, root cause analysis and quantifying the gap/opportunity in place?
<--- Score

13. Think about the functions involved in your Integrated Architecture Framework project, what processes flow from these functions?
<--- Score

14. What are the revised rough estimates of the financial savings/opportunity for Integrated Architecture Framework improvements?
<--- Score

15. What, related to, Integrated Architecture Framework processes does your organization outsource?
<--- Score

16. Has an output goal been set?
<--- Score

17. What is the output?
<--- Score

18. Has data output been validated?
<--- Score

19. Was a cause-and-effect diagram used to explore the different types of causes (or sources of variation)?
<--- Score

20. Is the final output clearly identified?

<--- Score

21. Was a detailed process map created to amplify critical steps of the 'as is' stakeholder process?
<--- Score

22. How do you define collaboration and team output?
<--- Score

23. What are the best opportunities for value improvement?
<--- Score

24. Is there a strict change management process?
<--- Score

25. Where is the data coming from to measure compliance?
<--- Score

26. What qualifications are necessary?
<--- Score

27. Do your contracts/agreements contain data security obligations?
<--- Score

28. How was the detailed process map generated, verified, and validated?
<--- Score

29. What tools were used to generate the list of possible causes?
<--- Score

30. What is the complexity of the output produced?
<--- Score

31. How do your work systems and key work processes relate to and capitalize on your core competencies?
<--- Score

32. How is the Integrated Architecture Framework Value Stream Mapping managed?
<--- Score

33. What methods do you use to gather Integrated Architecture Framework data?
<--- Score

34. What did the team gain from developing a sub-process map?
<--- Score

35. Do quality systems drive continuous improvement?
<--- Score

36. What is the cost of poor quality as supported by the team's analysis?
<--- Score

37. What qualifications and skills do you need?
<--- Score

38. What are your Integrated Architecture Framework processes?
<--- Score

39. Were there any improvement opportunities

identified from the process analysis?
<--- Score

40. How is the data gathered?
<--- Score

41. What resources go in to get the desired output?
<--- Score

42. What quality tools were used to get through the analyze phase?
<--- Score

43. What were the crucial 'moments of truth' on the process map?
<--- Score

44. What process should you select for improvement?
<--- Score

45. Were any designed experiments used to generate additional insight into the data analysis?
<--- Score

46. What are your current levels and trends in key Integrated Architecture Framework measures or indicators of product and process performance that are important to and directly serve your customers?
<--- Score

47. How difficult is it to qualify what Integrated Architecture Framework ROI is?
<--- Score

48. Who qualifies to gain access to data?

<--- Score

49. What were the financial benefits resulting from any 'ground fruit or low-hanging fruit' (quick fixes)?
<--- Score

50. Is the gap/opportunity displayed and communicated in financial terms?
<--- Score

51. What Integrated Architecture Framework data do you gather or use now?
<--- Score

52. How will corresponding data be collected?
<--- Score

53. What information qualified as important?
<--- Score

54. Are Integrated Architecture Framework changes recognized early enough to be approved through the regular process?
<--- Score

55. What qualifications are needed?
<--- Score

56. How much data can be collected in the given timeframe?
<--- Score

57. How do you use Integrated Architecture Framework data and information to support organizational decision making and innovation?
<--- Score

58. Is the performance gap determined?
<--- Score

59. How do you identify specific Integrated Architecture Framework investment opportunities and emerging trends?
<--- Score

60. How will the change process be managed?
<--- Score

61. Is pre-qualification of suppliers carried out?
<--- Score

62. Do your leaders quickly bounce back from setbacks?
<--- Score

63. Do your employees have the opportunity to do what they do best everyday?
<--- Score

64. How can risk management be tied procedurally to process elements?
<--- Score

65. What qualifications do Integrated Architecture Framework leaders need?
<--- Score

66. Do you, as a leader, bounce back quickly from setbacks?
<--- Score

67. Do you have the authority to produce the output?

<--- Score

68. What successful thing are you doing today that may be blinding you to new growth opportunities?
<--- Score

69. What are the necessary qualifications?
<--- Score

70. What are evaluation criteria for the output?
<--- Score

71. What Integrated Architecture Framework data should be managed?
<--- Score

72. Where can you get qualified talent today?
<--- Score

73. Record-keeping requirements flow from the records needed as inputs, outputs, controls and for transformation of a Integrated Architecture Framework process, are the records needed as inputs to the Integrated Architecture Framework process available?
<--- Score

74. How will the Integrated Architecture Framework data be captured?
<--- Score

75. What will drive Integrated Architecture Framework change?
<--- Score

76. What training and qualifications will you need?

<--- Score

77. Who is involved in the management review process?
<--- Score

78. Which Integrated Architecture Framework data should be retained?
<--- Score

79. What qualifies as competition?
<--- Score

80. How are outputs preserved and protected?
<--- Score

81. Have the problem and goal statements been updated to reflect the additional knowledge gained from the analyze phase?
<--- Score

82. How do you measure the operational performance of your key work systems and processes, including productivity, cycle time, and other appropriate measures of process effectiveness, efficiency, and innovation?
<--- Score

83. What are your outputs?
<--- Score

84. What controls do you have in place to protect data?
<--- Score

85. Do staff qualifications match your project?

<--- Score

86. Is the suppliers process defined and controlled?
<--- Score

87. What are your key performance measures or indicators and in-process measures for the control and improvement of your Integrated Architecture Framework processes?
<--- Score

88. How is Integrated Architecture Framework data gathered?
<--- Score

89. What output to create?
<--- Score

90. Are all team members qualified for all tasks?
<--- Score

91. What are the processes for audit reporting and management?
<--- Score

92. Is there an established change management process?
<--- Score

93. What are your current levels and trends in key measures or indicators of Integrated Architecture Framework product and process performance that are important to and directly serve your customers? How do these results compare with the performance of your competitors and other organizations with similar offerings?

<--- Score

94. Is the Integrated Architecture Framework process severely broken such that a re-design is necessary?
<--- Score

95. Who will gather what data?
<--- Score

96. What are the disruptive Integrated Architecture Framework technologies that enable your organization to radically change your business processes?
<--- Score

97. How do you ensure that the Integrated Architecture Framework opportunity is realistic?
<--- Score

98. How do mission and objectives affect the Integrated Architecture Framework processes of your organization?
<--- Score

99. What systems/processes must you excel at?
<--- Score

100. Who owns what data?
<--- Score

101. Are you missing Integrated Architecture Framework opportunities?
<--- Score

102. Were Pareto charts (or similar) used to portray the 'heavy hitters' (or key sources of variation)?

<--- Score

103. What are the personnel training and qualifications required?
<--- Score

104. What does the data say about the performance of the stakeholder process?
<--- Score

105. What do you need to qualify?
<--- Score

106. How do you promote understanding that opportunity for improvement is not criticism of the status quo, or the people who created the status quo?
<--- Score

107. Did any additional data need to be collected?
<--- Score

108. Who gets your output?
<--- Score

109. A compounding model resolution with available relevant data can often provide insight towards a solution methodology; which Integrated Architecture Framework models, tools and techniques are necessary?
<--- Score

110. Who is involved with workflow mapping?
<--- Score

111. What is the Integrated Architecture Framework Driver?

<--- Score

112. Are all staff in core Integrated Architecture Framework subjects Highly Qualified?
<--- Score

113. How often will data be collected for measures?
<--- Score

114. Have any additional benefits been identified that will result from closing all or most of the gaps?
<--- Score

115. How has the Integrated Architecture Framework data been gathered?
<--- Score

116. Are your outputs consistent?
<--- Score

117. How will the data be checked for quality?
<--- Score

118. What are your best practices for minimizing Integrated Architecture Framework project risk, while demonstrating incremental value and quick wins throughout the Integrated Architecture Framework project lifecycle?
<--- Score

119. What other jobs or tasks affect the performance of the steps in the Integrated Architecture Framework process?
<--- Score

120. What data do you need to collect?
<--- Score

121. Did any value-added analysis or 'lean thinking' take place to identify some of the gaps shown on the 'as is' process map?
<--- Score

122. Think about some of the processes you undertake within your organization, which do you own?
<--- Score

123. What tools were used to narrow the list of possible causes?
<--- Score

124. What is your organizations process which leads to recognition of value generation?
<--- Score

125. What Integrated Architecture Framework data should be collected?
<--- Score

126. What is the oversight process?
<--- Score

127. What kind of crime could a potential new hire have committed that would not only not disqualify him/her from being hired by your organization, but would actually indicate that he/she might be a particularly good fit?
<--- Score

128. Who will facilitate the team and process?

<--- Score

129. Are gaps between current performance and the goal performance identified?
<--- Score

130. How do you implement and manage your work processes to ensure that they meet design requirements?
<--- Score

Add up total points for this section:
_____ = Total points for this section

Divided by: _____ (number of statements answered) = _____
Average score for this section

Transfer your score to the Integrated Architecture Framework Index at the beginning of the Self-Assessment.

CRITERION #5: IMPROVE:

INTENT: Develop a practical solution. Innovate, establish and test the solution and to measure the results.

In my belief, the answer to this question is clearly defined:

5 Strongly Agree

4 Agree

3 Neutral

2 Disagree

1 Strongly Disagree

1. Is supporting Integrated Architecture Framework documentation required?
<--- Score

2. What went well, what should change, what can improve?
<--- Score

3. Can the solution be designed and implemented

within an acceptable time period?
<--- Score

4. How are Integrated Architecture Framework risks managed?
<--- Score

5. What are the expected Integrated Architecture Framework results?
<--- Score

6. Was a pilot designed for the proposed solution(s)?
<--- Score

7. What tools were most useful during the improve phase?
<--- Score

8. Is any Integrated Architecture Framework documentation required?
<--- Score

9. Who will be using the results of the measurement activities?
<--- Score

10. Who makes the Integrated Architecture Framework decisions in your organization?
<--- Score

11. Were any criteria developed to assist the team in testing and evaluating potential solutions?
<--- Score

12. Who should make the Integrated Architecture Framework decisions?

<--- Score

13. Does a good decision guarantee a good outcome?
<--- Score

14. What can you do to improve?
<--- Score

15. Is risk periodically assessed?
<--- Score

16. At what point will vulnerability assessments be performed once Integrated Architecture Framework is put into production (e.g., ongoing Risk Management after implementation)?
<--- Score

17. Are the risks fully understood, reasonable and manageable?
<--- Score

18. Who will be responsible for making the decisions to include or exclude requested changes once Integrated Architecture Framework is underway?
<--- Score

19. Do vendor agreements bring new compliance risk ?
<--- Score

20. Have you identified breakpoints and/or risk tolerances that will trigger broad consideration of a potential need for intervention or modification of strategy?

<--- Score

21. How is continuous improvement applied to risk management?
<--- Score

22. How can you improve Integrated Architecture Framework?
<--- Score

23. What is Integrated Architecture Framework's impact on utilizing the best solution(s)?
<--- Score

24. What attendant changes will need to be made to ensure that the solution is successful?
<--- Score

25. Is there a high likelihood that any recommendations will achieve their intended results?
<--- Score

26. How do you improve Integrated Architecture Framework service perception, and satisfaction?
<--- Score

27. What to do with the results or outcomes of measurements?
<--- Score

28. What are the implications of the one critical Integrated Architecture Framework decision 10 minutes, 10 months, and 10 years from now?
<--- Score

29. What is the risk?

<--- Score

30. How do you improve productivity?
<--- Score

31. Is the measure of success for Integrated Architecture Framework understandable to a variety of people?
<--- Score

32. Who are the key stakeholders for the Integrated Architecture Framework evaluation?
<--- Score

33. Is Integrated Architecture Framework documentation maintained?
<--- Score

34. Risk Identification: What are the possible risk events your organization faces in relation to Integrated Architecture Framework?
<--- Score

35. What are the concrete Integrated Architecture Framework results?
<--- Score

36. What lessons, if any, from a pilot were incorporated into the design of the full-scale solution?
<--- Score

37. Who manages Integrated Architecture Framework risk?
<--- Score

38. How scalable is your Integrated Architecture

Framework solution?
<--- Score

39. What practices helps your organization to develop its capacity to recognize patterns?
<--- Score

40. What alternative responses are available to manage risk?
<--- Score

41. Is the Integrated Architecture Framework documentation thorough?
<--- Score

42. What Integrated Architecture Framework improvements can be made?
<--- Score

43. How will you measure the results?
<--- Score

44. Who manages supplier risk management in your organization?
<--- Score

45. Who are the people involved in developing and implementing Integrated Architecture Framework?
<--- Score

46. Will the controls trigger any other risks?
<--- Score

47. How do you mitigate Integrated Architecture Framework risk?
<--- Score

48. Where do the Integrated Architecture Framework decisions reside?

<--- Score

49. What tools were used to tap into the creativity and encourage 'outside the box' thinking?

<--- Score

50. How will you know that you have improved?

<--- Score

51. How can you better manage risk?

<--- Score

52. How do you keep improving Integrated Architecture Framework?

<--- Score

53. How will you know when its improved?

<--- Score

54. Who controls the risk?

<--- Score

55. What tools were used to evaluate the potential solutions?

<--- Score

56. What is Integrated Architecture Framework risk?

<--- Score

57. What do you want to improve?

<--- Score

58. Which Integrated Architecture Framework solution

is appropriate?

<--- Score

59. How is knowledge sharing about risk management improved?

<--- Score

60. What is the implementation plan?

<--- Score

61. Who are the Integrated Architecture Framework decision makers?

<--- Score

62. Is the scope clearly documented?

<--- Score

63. Risk factors: what are the characteristics of Integrated Architecture Framework that make it risky?

<--- Score

64. How do you manage and improve your Integrated Architecture Framework work systems to deliver customer value and achieve organizational success and sustainability?

<--- Score

65. What were the criteria for evaluating a Integrated Architecture Framework pilot?

<--- Score

66. How will you know that a change is an improvement?

<--- Score

67. Do those selected for the Integrated Architecture Framework team have a good general understanding of what Integrated Architecture Framework is all about?
<--- Score

68. Where do you need Integrated Architecture Framework improvement?
<--- Score

69. Can you identify any significant risks or exposures to Integrated Architecture Framework third- parties (vendors, service providers, alliance partners etc) that concern you?
<--- Score

70. How do you improve your likelihood of success ?
<--- Score

71. Why improve in the first place?
<--- Score

72. Are events managed to resolution?
<--- Score

73. How are policy decisions made and where?
<--- Score

74. Which of the recognised risks out of all risks can be most likely transferred?
<--- Score

75. Is the solution technically practical?
<--- Score

76. What error proofing will be done to address some

of the discrepancies observed in the 'as is' process?
<--- Score

77. What is the magnitude of the improvements?
<--- Score

78. Who controls key decisions that will be made?
<--- Score

79. For estimation problems, how do you develop an estimation statement?
<--- Score

80. In the past few months, what is the smallest change you have made that has had the biggest positive result? What was it about that small change that produced the large return?
<--- Score

81. What tools do you use once you have decided on a Integrated Architecture Framework strategy and more importantly how do you choose?
<--- Score

82. For decision problems, how do you develop a decision statement?
<--- Score

83. How do the Integrated Architecture Framework results compare with the performance of your competitors and other organizations with similar offerings?
<--- Score

84. How do you go about comparing Integrated Architecture Framework approaches/solutions?

<--- Score

85. What actually has to improve and by how much?

<--- Score

86. Risk events: what are the things that could go wrong?

<--- Score

87. What current systems have to be understood and/or changed?

<--- Score

88. How risky is your organization?

<--- Score

89. Who do you report Integrated Architecture Framework results to?

<--- Score

90. What needs improvement? Why?

<--- Score

91. Explorations of the frontiers of Integrated Architecture Framework will help you build influence, improve Integrated Architecture Framework, optimize decision making, and sustain change, what is your approach?

<--- Score

92. What is the Integrated Architecture Framework's sustainability risk?

<--- Score

93. Who will be responsible for documenting the

Integrated Architecture Framework requirements in detail?

<--- Score

94. Are procedures documented for managing Integrated Architecture Framework risks?

<--- Score

95. How can the phases of Integrated Architecture Framework development be identified?

<--- Score

96. What strategies for Integrated Architecture Framework improvement are successful?

<--- Score

97. What are your current levels and trends in key measures or indicators of workforce and leader development?

<--- Score

98. How do you link measurement and risk?

<--- Score

99. What should a proof of concept or pilot accomplish?

<--- Score

100. How do you define the solutions' scope?

<--- Score

101. What area needs the greatest improvement?

<--- Score

102. Are you assessing Integrated Architecture Framework and risk?

<--- Score

103. Are decisions made in a timely manner?
<--- Score

104. How does your organization evaluate strategic Integrated Architecture Framework success?
<--- Score

105. If you could go back in time five years, what decision would you make differently? What is your best guess as to what decision you're making today you might regret five years from now?
<--- Score

106. Was a Integrated Architecture Framework charter developed?
<--- Score

107. What does the 'should be' process map/design look like?
<--- Score

108. How will you recognize and celebrate results?
<--- Score

109. What were the underlying assumptions on the cost-benefit analysis?
<--- Score

110. Would you develop a Integrated Architecture Framework Communication Strategy?
<--- Score

111. What are the affordable Integrated Architecture Framework risks?

<--- Score

112. Integrated Architecture Framework risk decisions: whose call Is It?
<--- Score

113. Do you combine technical expertise with business knowledge and Integrated Architecture Framework Key topics include lifecycles, development approaches, requirements and how to make a business case?
<--- Score

114. To what extent does management recognize Integrated Architecture Framework as a tool to increase the results?
<--- Score

115. What are the Integrated Architecture Framework security risks?
<--- Score

116. How can you improve performance?
<--- Score

117. Have you achieved Integrated Architecture Framework improvements?
<--- Score

118. What criteria will you use to assess your Integrated Architecture Framework risks?
<--- Score

119. When you map the key players in your own work and the types/domains of relationships with them, which relationships do you find easy and which

challenging, and why?
<--- Score

120. How do you decide how much to remunerate an employee?
<--- Score

121. What is the team's contingency plan for potential problems occurring in implementation?
<--- Score

122. Is the Integrated Architecture Framework solution sustainable?
<--- Score

123. Does the goal represent a desired result that can be measured?
<--- Score

124. How do you measure progress and evaluate training effectiveness?
<--- Score

125. How can skill-level changes improve Integrated Architecture Framework?
<--- Score

126. Do you cover the five essential competencies: Communication, Collaboration,Innovation, Adaptability, and Leadership that improve an organizations ability to leverage the new Integrated Architecture Framework in a volatile global economy?
<--- Score

127. What improvements have been achieved?
<--- Score

128. What communications are necessary to support the implementation of the solution?
<--- Score

129. What assumptions are made about the solution and approach?
<--- Score

130. How do you manage Integrated Architecture Framework risk?
<--- Score

131. Do you have the optimal project management team structure?
<--- Score

Add up total points for this section:
_ _ _ _ _ = Total points for this section

Divided by: _ _ _ _ _ _ (number of statements answered) = _ _ _ _ _ _
Average score for this section

Transfer your score to the Integrated Architecture Framework Index at the beginning of the Self-Assessment.

CRITERION #6: CONTROL:

INTENT: Implement the practical solution. Maintain the performance and correct possible complications.

In my belief, the answer to this question is clearly defined:

5 Strongly Agree

4 Agree

3 Neutral

2 Disagree

1 Strongly Disagree

1. Who is the Integrated Architecture Framework process owner?
<--- Score

2. Who will be in control?
<--- Score

3. What do your reports reflect?
<--- Score

4. Who is going to spread your message?
<--- Score

5. How do your controls stack up?
<--- Score

6. How do you plan for the cost of succession?
<--- Score

7. What adjustments to the strategies are needed?
<--- Score

8. Are the Integrated Architecture Framework standards challenging?
<--- Score

9. Is a response plan in place for when the input, process, or output measures indicate an 'out-of-control' condition?
<--- Score

10. What Integrated Architecture Framework standards are applicable?
<--- Score

11. How do you plan on providing proper recognition and disclosure of supporting companies?
<--- Score

12. How likely is the current Integrated Architecture Framework plan to come in on schedule or on budget?
<--- Score

13. What should you measure to verify efficiency gains?
<--- Score

14. What is the best design framework for Integrated Architecture Framework organization now that, in a post industrial-age if the top-down, command and control model is no longer relevant?
<--- Score

15. How do you encourage people to take control and responsibility?
<--- Score

16. How will the process owner and team be able to hold the gains?
<--- Score

17. How will new or emerging customer needs/ requirements be checked/communicated to orient the process toward meeting the new specifications and continually reducing variation?
<--- Score

18. Do you monitor the effectiveness of your Integrated Architecture Framework activities?
<--- Score

19. Who has control over resources?
<--- Score

20. What are you attempting to measure/monitor?
<--- Score

21. Do you monitor the Integrated Architecture Framework decisions made and fine tune them as

they evolve?
<--- Score

22. How do you spread information?
<--- Score

23. Is reporting being used or needed?
<--- Score

24. What quality tools were useful in the control phase?
<--- Score

25. Is the Integrated Architecture Framework test/ monitoring cost justified?
<--- Score

26. Is there documentation that will support the successful operation of the improvement?
<--- Score

27. How do you monitor usage and cost?
<--- Score

28. Do the viable solutions scale to future needs?
<--- Score

29. Act/Adjust: What Do you Need to Do Differently?
<--- Score

30. What other systems, operations, processes, and infrastructures (hiring practices, staffing, training, incentives/rewards, metrics/dashboards/scorecards, etc.) need updates, additions, changes, or deletions in order to facilitate knowledge transfer and improvements?

<--- Score

31. Is a response plan established and deployed?
<--- Score

32. How will report readings be checked to effectively monitor performance?
<--- Score

33. Do the Integrated Architecture Framework decisions you make today help people and the planet tomorrow?
<--- Score

34. Have new or revised work instructions resulted?
<--- Score

35. What are the critical parameters to watch?
<--- Score

36. What is your plan to assess your security risks?
<--- Score

37. How will Integrated Architecture Framework decisions be made and monitored?
<--- Score

38. How is change control managed?
<--- Score

39. How will the process owner verify improvement in present and future sigma levels, process capabilities?
<--- Score

40. Does the response plan contain a definite closed loop continual improvement scheme (e.g., plan-do-

check-act)?
<--- Score

41. How is Integrated Architecture Framework project cost planned, managed, monitored?
<--- Score

42. Does a troubleshooting guide exist or is it needed?
<--- Score

43. Is there a control plan in place for sustaining improvements (short and long-term)?
<--- Score

44. Will the team be available to assist members in planning investigations?
<--- Score

45. Can support from partners be adjusted?
<--- Score

46. Will existing staff require re-training, for example, to learn new business processes?
<--- Score

47. Are the planned controls in place?
<--- Score

48. What other areas of the group might benefit from the Integrated Architecture Framework team's improvements, knowledge, and learning?
<--- Score

49. Does job training on the documented procedures need to be part of the process team's education and training?

<--- Score

50. Are controls in place and consistently applied?
<--- Score

51. In the case of a Integrated Architecture Framework project, the criteria for the audit derive from implementation objectives, an audit of a Integrated Architecture Framework project involves assessing whether the recommendations outlined for implementation have been met, can you track that any Integrated Architecture Framework project is implemented as planned, and is it working?
<--- Score

52. Is there a documented and implemented monitoring plan?
<--- Score

53. Will any special training be provided for results interpretation?
<--- Score

54. What is the standard for acceptable Integrated Architecture Framework performance?
<--- Score

55. Can you adapt and adjust to changing Integrated Architecture Framework situations?
<--- Score

56. What can you control?
<--- Score

57. How do you select, collect, align, and integrate Integrated Architecture Framework data and

information for tracking daily operations and overall organizational performance, including progress relative to strategic objectives and action plans?
<--- Score

58. Are new process steps, standards, and documentation ingrained into normal operations?
<--- Score

59. Is there a Integrated Architecture Framework Communication plan covering who needs to get what information when?
<--- Score

60. Are suggested corrective/restorative actions indicated on the response plan for known causes to problems that might surface?
<--- Score

61. Has the Integrated Architecture Framework value of standards been quantified?
<--- Score

62. How widespread is its use?
<--- Score

63. How do controls support value?
<--- Score

64. Is there a transfer of ownership and knowledge to process owner and process team tasked with the responsibilities.
<--- Score

65. What are customers monitoring?
<--- Score

66. What do you stand for--and what are you against?

<--- Score

67. Is knowledge gained on process shared and institutionalized?

<--- Score

68. How will you measure your QA plan's effectiveness?

<--- Score

69. How might the group capture best practices and lessons learned so as to leverage improvements?

<--- Score

70. What key inputs and outputs are being measured on an ongoing basis?

<--- Score

71. What are the known security controls?

<--- Score

72. What are the performance and scale of the Integrated Architecture Framework tools?

<--- Score

73. What are your results for key measures or indicators of the accomplishment of your Integrated Architecture Framework strategy and action plans, including building and strengthening core competencies?

<--- Score

74. What is your theory of human motivation, and

how does your compensation plan fit with that view?

<--- Score

75. Are documented procedures clear and easy to follow for the operators?

<--- Score

76. What is the control/monitoring plan?

<--- Score

77. How do you establish and deploy modified action plans if circumstances require a shift in plans and rapid execution of new plans?

<--- Score

78. Who sets the Integrated Architecture Framework standards?

<--- Score

79. How will input, process, and output variables be checked to detect for sub-optimal conditions?

<--- Score

80. Has the improved process and its steps been standardized?

<--- Score

81. Is there a recommended audit plan for routine surveillance inspections of Integrated Architecture Framework's gains?

<--- Score

82. How will the day-to-day responsibilities for monitoring and continual improvement be transferred from the improvement team to the

process owner?
<--- Score

83. How do senior leaders actions reflect a commitment to the organizations Integrated Architecture Framework values?
<--- Score

84. Is there an action plan in case of emergencies?
<--- Score

85. Is new knowledge gained imbedded in the response plan?
<--- Score

86. What are the key elements of your Integrated Architecture Framework performance improvement system, including your evaluation, organizational learning, and innovation processes?
<--- Score

87. You may have created your quality measures at a time when you lacked resources, technology wasn't up to the required standard, or low service levels were the industry norm. Have those circumstances changed?
<--- Score

88. Are the planned controls working?
<--- Score

89. Does the Integrated Architecture Framework performance meet the customer's requirements?
<--- Score

90. Are pertinent alerts monitored, analyzed and

distributed to appropriate personnel?
<--- Score

91. Where do ideas that reach policy makers and planners as proposals for Integrated Architecture Framework strengthening and reform actually originate?
<--- Score

92. Will your goals reflect your program budget?
<--- Score

93. Are operating procedures consistent?
<--- Score

94. Does Integrated Architecture Framework appropriately measure and monitor risk?
<--- Score

95. What is the recommended frequency of auditing?
<--- Score

96. What should the next improvement project be that is related to Integrated Architecture Framework?
<--- Score

97. What do you measure to verify effectiveness gains?
<--- Score

98. Implementation Planning: is a pilot needed to test the changes before a full roll out occurs?
<--- Score

99. How can you best use all of your knowledge repositories to enhance learning and sharing?

<--- Score

100. Are there documented procedures?
<--- Score

101. Who controls critical resources?
<--- Score

102. Is there a standardized process?
<--- Score

Add up total points for this section:
_ _ _ _ _ = Total points for this section

Divided by: _ _ _ _ _ _ (number of
statements answered) = _ _ _ _ _ _
Average score for this section

Transfer your score to the Integrated
Architecture Framework Index at the
beginning of the Self-Assessment.

CRITERION #7: SUSTAIN:

INTENT: Retain the benefits.

In my belief, the answer to this question is clearly defined:

5 Strongly Agree

4 Agree

3 Neutral

2 Disagree

1 Strongly Disagree

1. How do you set Integrated Architecture Framework stretch targets and how do you get people to not only participate in setting these stretch targets but also that they strive to achieve these?
<--- Score

2. Do you know what you are doing? And who do you call if you don't?
<--- Score

3. What is your BATNA (best alternative to a negotiated agreement)?

<--- Score

4. How will you insure seamless interoperability of Integrated Architecture Framework moving forward?

<--- Score

5. Are new benefits received and understood?

<--- Score

6. Is a Integrated Architecture Framework team work effort in place?

<--- Score

7. Is there any reason to believe the opposite of my current belief?

<--- Score

8. What is your formula for success in Integrated Architecture Framework ?

<--- Score

9. What potential megatrends could make your business model obsolete?

<--- Score

10. How are you doing compared to your industry?

<--- Score

11. Where can you break convention?

<--- Score

12. What would you recommend your friend do if he/she were facing this dilemma?

<--- Score

13. Who uses your product in ways you never expected?
<--- Score

14. In a project to restructure Integrated Architecture Framework outcomes, which stakeholders would you involve?
<--- Score

15. What happens when a new employee joins the organization?
<--- Score

16. Who else should you help?
<--- Score

17. What is your Integrated Architecture Framework strategy?
<--- Score

18. How do you stay inspired?
<--- Score

19. Which Integrated Architecture Framework goals are the most important?
<--- Score

20. How do you proactively clarify deliverables and Integrated Architecture Framework quality expectations?
<--- Score

21. How do you provide a safe environment -physically and emotionally?

<--- Score

22. Ask yourself: how would you do this work if you only had one staff member to do it?
<--- Score

23. What are your most important goals for the strategic Integrated Architecture Framework objectives?
<--- Score

24. Who do you want your customers to become?
<--- Score

25. Is Integrated Architecture Framework dependent on the successful delivery of a current project?
<--- Score

26. What is your question? Why?
<--- Score

27. Think of your Integrated Architecture Framework project, what are the main functions?
<--- Score

28. How do you cross-sell and up-sell your Integrated Architecture Framework success?
<--- Score

29. What is the purpose of Integrated Architecture Framework in relation to the mission?
<--- Score

30. How do you manage Integrated Architecture Framework Knowledge Management (KM)?
<--- Score

31. Are you making progress, and are you making progress as Integrated Architecture Framework leaders?
<--- Score

32. Do you know who is a friend or a foe?
<--- Score

33. What knowledge, skills and characteristics mark a good Integrated Architecture Framework project manager?
<--- Score

34. What management system can you use to leverage the Integrated Architecture Framework experience, ideas, and concerns of the people closest to the work to be done?
<--- Score

35. What is the recommended frequency of auditing?
<--- Score

36. If no one would ever find out about your accomplishments, how would you lead differently?
<--- Score

37. How will you motivate the stakeholders with the least vested interest?
<--- Score

38. Are there any activities that you can take off your to do list?
<--- Score

39. How will you know that the Integrated

Architecture Framework project has been successful?

<--- Score

40. If you find that you havent accomplished one of the goals for one of the steps of the Integrated Architecture Framework strategy, what will you do to fix it?

<--- Score

41. Do Integrated Architecture Framework rules make a reasonable demand on a users capabilities?

<--- Score

42. What you are going to do to affect the numbers?

<--- Score

43. What are the short and long-term Integrated Architecture Framework goals?

<--- Score

44. Who will manage the integration of tools?

<--- Score

45. Do you think Integrated Architecture Framework accomplishes the goals you expect it to accomplish?

<--- Score

46. Do you think you know, or do you know you know ?

<--- Score

47. Who are four people whose careers you have enhanced?

<--- Score

48. What is the craziest thing you can do?

<--- Score

49. Have new benefits been realized?

<--- Score

50. Which models, tools and techniques are necessary?

<--- Score

51. Who will determine interim and final deadlines?

<--- Score

52. What relationships among Integrated Architecture Framework trends do you perceive?

<--- Score

53. How can you become the company that would put you out of business?

<--- Score

54. Are you changing as fast as the world around you?

<--- Score

55. Who will provide the final approval of Integrated Architecture Framework deliverables?

<--- Score

56. Who, on the executive team or the board, has spoken to a customer recently?

<--- Score

57. What happens at your organization when people fail?

<--- Score

58. Are the assumptions believable and achievable?
<--- Score

59. What is the range of capabilities?
<--- Score

60. Are you using a design thinking approach and integrating Innovation, Integrated Architecture Framework Experience, and Brand Value?
<--- Score

61. What must you excel at?
<--- Score

62. Is Integrated Architecture Framework realistic, or are you setting yourself up for failure?
<--- Score

63. What are the potential basics of Integrated Architecture Framework fraud?
<--- Score

64. Would you rather sell to knowledgeable and informed customers or to uninformed customers?
<--- Score

65. How will you ensure you get what you expected?
<--- Score

66. Political -is anyone trying to undermine this project?
<--- Score

67. Do you have the right people on the bus?

<--- Score

68. What is the estimated value of the project?
<--- Score

69. Why is Integrated Architecture Framework important for you now?
<--- Score

70. What are the barriers to increased Integrated Architecture Framework production?
<--- Score

71. Did your employees make progress today?
<--- Score

72. What information is critical to your organization that your executives are ignoring?
<--- Score

73. If you weren't already in this business, would you enter it today? And if not, what are you going to do about it?
<--- Score

74. What business benefits will Integrated Architecture Framework goals deliver if achieved?
<--- Score

75. How does Integrated Architecture Framework integrate with other stakeholder initiatives?
<--- Score

76. If you were responsible for initiating and implementing major changes in your organization, what steps might you take to ensure acceptance of

those changes?
<--- Score

77. How do you foster innovation?
<--- Score

78. Will there be any necessary staff changes (redundancies or new hires)?
<--- Score

79. How do you foster the skills, knowledge, talents, attributes, and characteristics you want to have?
<--- Score

80. How do you know if you are successful?
<--- Score

81. What is your competitive advantage?
<--- Score

82. Who will be responsible for deciding whether Integrated Architecture Framework goes ahead or not after the initial investigations?
<--- Score

83. What would have to be true for the option on the table to be the best possible choice?
<--- Score

84. What are the usability implications of Integrated Architecture Framework actions?
<--- Score

85. How important is Integrated Architecture Framework to the user organizations mission?
<--- Score

86. What role does communication play in the success or failure of a Integrated Architecture Framework project?
<--- Score

87. What have been your experiences in defining long range Integrated Architecture Framework goals?
<--- Score

88. What trophy do you want on your mantle?
<--- Score

89. Is your strategy driving your strategy? Or is the way in which you allocate resources driving your strategy?
<--- Score

90. What Integrated Architecture Framework modifications can you make work for you?
<--- Score

91. Are all key stakeholders present at all Structured Walkthroughs?
<--- Score

92. What goals did you miss?
<--- Score

93. Is maximizing Integrated Architecture Framework protection the same as minimizing Integrated Architecture Framework loss?
<--- Score

94. If you had to rebuild your organization without any traditional competitive advantages (i.e., no killer

technology, promising research, innovative product/ service delivery model, etcetera), how would your people have to approach their work and collaborate together in order to create the necessary conditions for success?
<--- Score

95. Do you have an implicit bias for capital investments over people investments?
<--- Score

96. Instead of going to current contacts for new ideas, what if you reconnected with dormant contacts-- the people you used to know? If you were going reactivate a dormant tie, who would it be?
<--- Score

97. What Integrated Architecture Framework skills are most important?
<--- Score

98. Who is on the team?
<--- Score

99. Are you / should you be revolutionary or evolutionary?
<--- Score

100. What is the overall talent health of your organization as a whole at senior levels, and for each organization reporting to a member of the Senior Leadership Team?
<--- Score

101. What are the gaps in your knowledge and experience?

<--- Score

102. If you do not follow, then how to lead?
<--- Score

103. How do you go about securing Integrated Architecture Framework?
<--- Score

104. How much does Integrated Architecture Framework help?
<--- Score

105. How do you ensure that implementations of Integrated Architecture Framework products are done in a way that ensures safety?
<--- Score

106. What is it like to work for you?
<--- Score

107. What are the essentials of internal Integrated Architecture Framework management?
<--- Score

108. What are the challenges?
<--- Score

109. How much contingency will be available in the budget?
<--- Score

110. How do you transition from the baseline to the target?
<--- Score

111. What are the business goals Integrated Architecture Framework is aiming to achieve?
<--- Score

112. Are you satisfied with your current role? If not, what is missing from it?
<--- Score

113. Who are your customers?
<--- Score

114. What threat is Integrated Architecture Framework addressing?
<--- Score

115. Why is it important to have senior management support for a Integrated Architecture Framework project?
<--- Score

116. What are current Integrated Architecture Framework paradigms?
<--- Score

117. How do you make it meaningful in connecting Integrated Architecture Framework with what users do day-to-day?
<--- Score

118. In retrospect, of the projects that you pulled the plug on, what percent do you wish had been allowed to keep going, and what percent do you wish had ended earlier?
<--- Score

119. How do you maintain Integrated Architecture

Framework's Integrity?
<--- Score

120. Operational - will it work?
<--- Score

121. How do you keep the momentum going?
<--- Score

122. Why should people listen to you?
<--- Score

123. How do you assess the Integrated Architecture Framework pitfalls that are inherent in implementing it?
<--- Score

124. Is the Integrated Architecture Framework organization completing tasks effectively and efficiently?
<--- Score

125. When information truly is ubiquitous, when reach and connectivity are completely global, when computing resources are infinite, and when a whole new set of impossibilities are not only possible, but happening, what will that do to your business?
<--- Score

126. Who is responsible for ensuring appropriate resources (time, people and money) are allocated to Integrated Architecture Framework?
<--- Score

127. What are the rules and assumptions your industry

operates under? What if the opposite were true?
<--- Score

128. What one word do you want to own in the minds of your customers, employees, and partners?
<--- Score

129. How likely is it that a customer would recommend your company to a friend or colleague?
<--- Score

130. Whom among your colleagues do you trust, and for what?
<--- Score

131. Who is the main stakeholder, with ultimate responsibility for driving Integrated Architecture Framework forward?
<--- Score

132. Who do you think the world wants your organization to be?
<--- Score

133. Is a Integrated Architecture Framework breakthrough on the horizon?
<--- Score

134. If you got fired and a new hire took your place, what would she do different?
<--- Score

135. Which individuals, teams or departments will be involved in Integrated Architecture Framework?
<--- Score

136. What does your signature ensure?
<--- Score

137. Will it be accepted by users?
<--- Score

138. If there were zero limitations, what would you do differently?
<--- Score

139. What are the key enablers to make this Integrated Architecture Framework move?
<--- Score

140. Can you do all this work?
<--- Score

141. What projects are going on in the organization today, and what resources are those projects using from the resource pools?
<--- Score

142. What are strategies for increasing support and reducing opposition?
<--- Score

143. Have benefits been optimized with all key stakeholders?
<--- Score

144. Why will customers want to buy your organizations products/services?
<--- Score

145. Are you maintaining a past–present–future perspective throughout the Integrated

Architecture Framework discussion?

<--- Score

146. Do you have the right capabilities and capacities?

<--- Score

147. Why should you adopt a Integrated Architecture Framework framework?

<--- Score

148. To whom do you add value?

<--- Score

149. What is the funding source for this project?

<--- Score

150. What new services of functionality will be implemented next with Integrated Architecture Framework ?

<--- Score

151. Can you maintain your growth without detracting from the factors that have contributed to your success?

<--- Score

152. What are the top 3 things at the forefront of your Integrated Architecture Framework agendas for the next 3 years?

<--- Score

153. What are you challenging?

<--- Score

154. Who are the key stakeholders?

<--- Score

155. Were lessons learned captured and communicated?
<--- Score

156. How do you track customer value, profitability or financial return, organizational success, and sustainability?
<--- Score

157. How do customers see your organization?
<--- Score

158. If your company went out of business tomorrow, would anyone who doesn't get a paycheck here care?
<--- Score

159. Which functions and people interact with the supplier and or customer?
<--- Score

160. What will be the consequences to the stakeholder (financial, reputation etc) if Integrated Architecture Framework does not go ahead or fails to deliver the objectives?
<--- Score

161. Can you break it down?
<--- Score

162. What are internal and external Integrated Architecture Framework relations?
<--- Score

163. Can the schedule be done in the given time?

<--- Score

164. If you had to leave your organization for a year and the only communication you could have with employees/colleagues was a single paragraph, what would you write?
<--- Score

165. What is something you believe that nearly no one agrees with you on?
<--- Score

166. How is implementation research currently incorporated into each of your goals?
<--- Score

167. Do you have enough freaky customers in your portfolio pushing you to the limit day in and day out?
<--- Score

168. At what moment would you think; Will I get fired?
<--- Score

169. What is the kind of project structure that would be appropriate for your Integrated Architecture Framework project, should it be formal and complex, or can it be less formal and relatively simple?
<--- Score

170. What is the overall business strategy?
<--- Score

171. What do we do when new problems arise?
<--- Score

172. How do you determine the key elements that affect Integrated Architecture Framework workforce satisfaction, how are these elements determined for different workforce groups and segments?
<--- Score

173. How do you govern and fulfill your societal responsibilities?
<--- Score

174. How do you keep records, of what?
<--- Score

175. What are the long-term Integrated Architecture Framework goals?
<--- Score

176. Are you relevant? Will you be relevant five years from now? Ten?
<--- Score

177. How do you accomplish your long range Integrated Architecture Framework goals?
<--- Score

178. Are your responses positive or negative?
<--- Score

179. What is an unauthorized commitment?
<--- Score

180. What happens if you do not have enough funding?
<--- Score

181. Why not do Integrated Architecture Framework?
<--- Score

182. Do you have past Integrated Architecture Framework successes?
<--- Score

183. How do you listen to customers to obtain actionable information?
<--- Score

184. Is there a work around that you can use?
<--- Score

185. What is the source of the strategies for Integrated Architecture Framework strengthening and reform?
<--- Score

186. Has implementation been effective in reaching specified objectives so far?
<--- Score

187. Do you see more potential in people than they do in themselves?
<--- Score

188. How do you lead with Integrated Architecture Framework in mind?
<--- Score

189. Is your basic point _____ or _____?
<--- Score

190. Who is responsible for errors?
<--- Score

191. How do you engage the workforce, in addition to satisfying them?
<--- Score

192. How can you incorporate support to ensure safe and effective use of Integrated Architecture Framework into the services that you provide?
<--- Score

193. Who is responsible for Integrated Architecture Framework?
<--- Score

194. What did you miss in the interview for the worst hire you ever made?
<--- Score

195. In the past year, what have you done (or could you have done) to increase the accurate perception of your company/brand as ethical and honest?
<--- Score

196. Is the impact that Integrated Architecture Framework has shown?
<--- Score

197. Marketing budgets are tighter, consumers are more skeptical, and social media has changed forever the way we talk about Integrated Architecture Framework, how do you gain traction?
<--- Score

198. Are you paying enough attention to the partners your company depends on to succeed?
<--- Score

199. What are you trying to prove to yourself, and how might it be hijacking your life and business success?

<--- Score

200. What is effective Integrated Architecture Framework?

<--- Score

201. Why do and why don't your customers like your organization?

<--- Score

202. Whose voice (department, ethnic group, women, older workers, etc) might you have missed hearing from in your company, and how might you amplify this voice to create positive momentum for your business?

<--- Score

203. Who do we want your customers to become?

<--- Score

204. What should you stop doing?

<--- Score

205. What stupid rule would you most like to kill?

<--- Score

206. What is the big Integrated Architecture Framework idea?

<--- Score

207. What could happen if you do not do it?

<--- Score

208. How do senior leaders deploy your organizations vision and values through your leadership system, to the workforce, to key suppliers and partners, and to customers and other stakeholders, as appropriate?
<--- Score

209. Do you say no to customers for no reason?
<--- Score

210. What may be the consequences for the performance of an organization if all stakeholders are not consulted regarding Integrated Architecture Framework?
<--- Score

211. What trouble can you get into?
<--- Score

212. Are assumptions made in Integrated Architecture Framework stated explicitly?
<--- Score

213. How can you negotiate Integrated Architecture Framework successfully with a stubborn boss, an irate client, or a deceitful coworker?
<--- Score

214. Is it economical; do you have the time and money?
<--- Score

215. What are the success criteria that will indicate that Integrated Architecture Framework objectives have been met and the benefits delivered?
<--- Score

216. How can you become more high-tech but still be high touch?

<--- Score

Add up total points for this section:
_____ = Total points for this section

Divided by: _____ (number of
statements answered) = _____
Average score for this section

Transfer your score to the Integrated
Architecture Framework Index at the
beginning of the Self-Assessment.

Integrated Architecture Framework and Managing Projects, Criteria for Project Managers:

1.0 Initiating Process Group: Integrated Architecture Framework

1. What were the challenges that you encountered during the execution of a previous Integrated Architecture Framework project that you would not want to repeat?

2. How will you do it?

3. Who supports, improves, and oversees standardized processes related to the Integrated Architecture Framework projects program?

4. First of all, should any action be taken?

5. What are the overarching issues of your organization?

6. Did you use a contractor or vendor?

7. The Integrated Architecture Framework project you are managing has nine stakeholders. How many channel of communications are there between corresponding stakeholders?

8. Will the Integrated Architecture Framework project meet the client requirements, and will it achieve the business success criteria that justified doing the Integrated Architecture Framework project in the first place?

9. Did the Integrated Architecture Framework project team have the right skills?

10. Do you know if the Integrated Architecture Framework project requires outside equipment or vendor resources?

11. How well did the chosen processes fit the needs of the Integrated Architecture Framework project?

12. Do you know all the stakeholders impacted by the Integrated Architecture Framework project and what needs are?

13. The process to Manage Stakeholders is part of which process group?

14. What will be the pressing issues of tomorrow?

15. What input will you be required to provide the Integrated Architecture Framework project team?

16. Professionals want to know what is expected from them what are the deliverables?

17. How will it affect me?

18. What are the required resources?

19. Are the changes in your Integrated Architecture Framework project being formally requested, analyzed, and approved by the appropriate decision makers?

20. What were things that you did well, and could improve, and how?

1.1 Project Charter: Integrated Architecture Framework

21. Why the improvements?

22. What are some examples of a business case?

23. Did your Integrated Architecture Framework project ask for this?

24. Why do you need to manage scope?

25. What date will the task finish?

26. For whom?

27. What outcome, in measureable terms, are you hoping to accomplish?

28. Are you building in-house ?

29. Run it as as a startup?

30. Why do you manage integration?

31. Who is the Integrated Architecture Framework project Manager?

32. Are there special technology requirements?

33. What are the assigned resources?

34. Why is it important?

35. Why have you chosen the aim you have set forth?

36. When is a charter needed?

37. What barriers do you predict to your success?

38. What are the assumptions?

39. Who will take notes, document decisions?

40. Integrated Architecture Framework project background: what is the primary motivation for this Integrated Architecture Framework project?

1.2 Stakeholder Register: Integrated Architecture Framework

41. How big is the gap?

42. How should employers make voices heard?

43. Who wants to talk about Security?

44. Is your organization ready for change?

45. How much influence do they have on the Integrated Architecture Framework project?

46. Who are the stakeholders?

47. What is the power of the stakeholder?

48. What are the major Integrated Architecture Framework project milestones requiring communications or providing communications opportunities?

49. Who is managing stakeholder engagement?

50. What & Why?

51. How will reports be created?

52. What opportunities exist to provide communications?

1.3 Stakeholder Analysis Matrix: Integrated Architecture Framework

53. Resources, assets, people?

54. How do they affect the Integrated Architecture Framework project and its outcomes?

55. Do the stakeholders goals and expectations support or conflict with the Integrated Architecture Framework project goals?

56. Do recommendations include actions to address any differential distribution of impacts?

57. Who will be affected by the Integrated Architecture Framework project?

58. Who are potential allies and opponents?

59. Who can contribute financial or technical resources towards the work?

60. Marketing - reach, distribution, awareness?

61. How will the stakeholder directly benefit from the Integrated Architecture Framework project and how will this affect the stakeholders motivation?

62. Does your organization have bad debt or cash-flow problems?

63. Market demand?

64. Market developments?

65. Business and product development?

66. What do you Evaluate?

67. Which conditions out of the control of the management are crucial for the sustainability of its effects?

68. How do rules, behaviors affect stakes?

69. Financial reserves, likely returns?

70. What is accountability in relation to the Integrated Architecture Framework project?

71. What should thwe organizations stakeholders avoid?

72. Are there different rules or organizational models for men and women?

2.0 Planning Process Group: Integrated Architecture Framework

73. How will users learn how to use the deliverables?

74. The Integrated Architecture Framework project charter is created in which Integrated Architecture Framework project management process group?

75. What will you do?

76. Explanation: is what the Integrated Architecture Framework project intents to solve a hard question?

77. Do the partners have sufficient financial capacity to keep up the benefits produced by the programme?

78. Mitigate. what will you do to minimize the impact should a risk event occur?

79. Product breakdown structure (pbs): what is the Integrated Architecture Framework project result or product, and how should it look like, what are its parts?

80. In what way has the program contributed towards the issue culture and development included on the public agenda?

81. To what extent have public/private national resources and/or counterparts been mobilized to contribute to the programs objective and produce results and impacts?

82. Did you read it correctly?

83. If task x starts two days late, what is the effect on the Integrated Architecture Framework project end date?

84. Will you be replaced?

85. Is the schedule for the set products being met?

86. To what extent are the participating departments coordinating with each other?

87. What is involved in Integrated Architecture Framework project scope management, and why is good Integrated Architecture Framework project scope management so important on information technology Integrated Architecture Framework projects?

88. What is the difference between the early schedule and late schedule?

89. To what extent and in what ways are the Integrated Architecture Framework project contributing to progress towards organizational reform?

90. Contingency planning. if a risk event occurs, what will you do?

91. Did the program design/ implementation strategy adequately address the planning stage necessary to set up structures, hire staff etc.?

2.1 Project Management Plan: Integrated Architecture Framework

92. How well are you able to manage your risk?

93. What are the training needs?

94. Do there need to be organizational changes?

95. Are there any windfall benefits that would accrue to the Integrated Architecture Framework project sponsor or other parties?

96. Is there an incremental analysis/cost effectiveness analysis of proposed mitigation features based on an approved method and using an accepted model?

97. How do you organize the costs in the Integrated Architecture Framework project management plan?

98. What went wrong?

99. Are the proposed Integrated Architecture Framework project purposes different than a previously authorized Integrated Architecture Framework project?

100. Did the planning effort collaborate to develop solutions that integrate expertise, policies, programs, and Integrated Architecture Framework projects across entities?

101. Will you add a schedule and diagram?

102. Are calculations and results of analyzes essentially correct?

103. Is mitigation authorized or recommended?

104. Are there any scope changes proposed for a previously authorized Integrated Architecture Framework project?

105. Was the peer (technical) review of the cost estimates duly coordinated with the cost estimate center of expertise and addressed in the review documentation and certification?

106. Do the proposed changes from the Integrated Architecture Framework project include any significant risks to safety?

107. What happened during the process that you found interesting?

108. Where does all this information come from?

109. If the Integrated Architecture Framework project management plan is a comprehensive document that guides you in Integrated Architecture Framework project execution and control, then what should it NOT contain?

110. Who is the sponsor?

2.2 Scope Management Plan: Integrated Architecture Framework

111. Have all necessary approvals been obtained?

112. Have external dependencies been captured in the schedule?

113. Is a pmo (Integrated Architecture Framework project management office) in place and provide oversight to the Integrated Architecture Framework project?

114. Can the Integrated Architecture Framework project team do several activities in parallel?

115. Has allowance been made for vacations, holidays, training (learning time for each team member), staff promotions & staff turnovers?

116. Are Integrated Architecture Framework project leaders committed to this Integrated Architecture Framework project full time?

117. Is your organization structure for both tracking & controlling the budget well defined and assigned to a specific individual?

118. Describe the manner in which Integrated Architecture Framework project deliverables will be formally presented and accepted. Will they be presented at the end of each phase?

119. Are schedule deliverables actually delivered?

120. What happens if scope changes?

121. Does the detailed work plan match the complexity of tasks with the capabilities of personnel?

122. Are you doing what you have set out to do?

123. Is documentation created for communication with the suppliers and Vendors?

124. When is corrective or preventative action required?

125. Are metrics used to evaluate and manage Vendors?

126. Is stakeholder involvement adequate?

127. What is the estimated cost of creating and implementing?

128. What are the risks that could significantly affect the communication on the Integrated Architecture Framework project?

129. Is there a Steering Committee in place?

130. What weaknesses do you have?

2.3 Requirements Management Plan: Integrated Architecture Framework

131. Is infrastructure setup part of your Integrated Architecture Framework project?

132. Should you include sub-activities?

133. Did you use declarative statements?

134. Who is responsible for monitoring and tracking the Integrated Architecture Framework project requirements?

135. Who came up with this requirement?

136. How knowledgeable is the primary Stakeholder(s) in the proposed application area?

137. Is there formal agreement on who has authority to request a change in requirements?

138. Will the product release be stable and mature enough to be deployed in the user community?

139. How knowledgeable is the team in the proposed application area?

140. Is the system software (non-operating system) new to the IT Integrated Architecture Framework project team?

141. Have stakeholders been instructed in the Change

Control process?

142. Subject to change control?

143. Who has the authority to reject Integrated Architecture Framework project requirements?

144. Business analysis scope?

145. What performance metrics will be used?

146. What is the earliest finish date for this Integrated Architecture Framework project if it is scheduled to start on ...?

147. Are all the stakeholders ready for the transition into the user community?

148. Is there formal agreement on who has authority to approve a change in requirements?

149. Who is responsible for quantifying the Integrated Architecture Framework project requirements?

2.4 Requirements Documentation: Integrated Architecture Framework

150. Consistency. are there any requirements conflicts?

151. What are the potential disadvantages/advantages?

152. How to document system requirements?

153. Is your business case still valid?

154. What are the acceptance criteria?

155. Where do system and software requirements come from, what are sources?

156. What is your Elevator Speech?

157. The problem with gathering requirements is right there in the word gathering. What images does it conjure?

158. What is a show stopper in the requirements?

159. Does your organization restrict technical alternatives?

160. What facilities must be supported by the system?

161. What can tools do for us?

162. Who provides requirements?

163. Verifiability. can the requirements be checked?

164. What is effective documentation?

165. Are all functions required by the customer included?

166. How will they be documented / shared?

167. Are there any requirements conflicts?

168. How will requirements be documented and who signs off on them?

169. What images does it conjure?

2.5 Requirements Traceability Matrix: Integrated Architecture Framework

170. How will it affect the stakeholders personally in career?

171. What is the WBS?

172. What percentage of Integrated Architecture Framework projects are producing traceability matrices between requirements and other work products?

173. How small is small enough?

174. Will you use a Requirements Traceability Matrix?

175. Do you have a clear understanding of all subcontracts in place?

176. What are the chronologies, contingencies, consequences, criteria?

177. How do you manage scope?

178. Is there a requirements traceability process in place?

179. Why use a WBS?

180. Why do you manage scope?

181. Describe the process for approving requirements

so they can be added to the traceability matrix and Integrated Architecture Framework project work can be performed. Will the Integrated Architecture Framework project requirements become approved in writing?

2.6 Project Scope Statement: Integrated Architecture Framework

182. Will an issue form be in use?

183. Will you need a statement of work?

184. If there are vendors, have they signed off on the Integrated Architecture Framework project Plan?

185. Relevant - ask yourself can you get there; why are you doing this Integrated Architecture Framework project?

186. Who will you recommend approve the change, and when do you recommend the change reviews occur?

187. Is this process communicated to the customer and team members?

188. Any new risks introduced or old risks impacted. Are there issues that could affect the existing requirements for the result, service, or product if the scope changes?

189. Is the scope of your Integrated Architecture Framework project well defined?

190. Will all tasks resulting from issues be entered into the Integrated Architecture Framework project Plan and tracked through the plan?

191. Has the format for tracking and monitoring schedules and costs been defined?

192. Is your organization structure appropriate for the Integrated Architecture Framework projects size and complexity?

193. Is there a Change Management Board?

194. Will the risk plan be updated on a regular and frequent basis?

195. If there is an independent oversight contractor, have they signed off on the Integrated Architecture Framework project Plan?

196. Have you been able to thoroughly document the Integrated Architecture Framework projects assumptions and constraints?

197. Integrated Architecture Framework project lead, team lead, solution architect?

198. Is there a process (test plans, inspections, reviews) defined for verifying outputs for each task?

199. Has the Integrated Architecture Framework project scope statement been reviewed as part of the baseline process?

200. Are the meetings set up to have assigned note takers that will add action/issues to the issue list?

201. What are the possible consequences should a risk come to occur?

2.7 Assumption and Constraint Log: Integrated Architecture Framework

202. What strengths do you have?

203. Security analysis has access to information that is sanitized?

204. What does an audit system look like?

205. Diagrams and tables are included to account for complex concepts and increase overall readability?

206. Are there ways to reduce the time it takes to get something approved?

207. Does a documented Integrated Architecture Framework project organizational policy & plan (i.e. governance model) exist?

208. What is positive about the current process?

209. Is the process working, and people are not executing in compliance of the process?

210. Are best practices and metrics employed to identify issues, progress, performance, etc.?

211. Is this model reasonable?

212. Can the requirements be traced to the appropriate components of the solution, as well as test scripts?

213. Are processes for release management of new development from coding and unit testing, to integration testing, to training, and production defined and followed?

214. Are there processes in place to ensure that all the terms and code concepts have been documented consistently?

215. Model-building: what data-analytic strategies are useful when building proportional-hazards models?

216. Is there documentation of system capability requirements, data requirements, environment requirements, security requirements, and computer and hardware requirements?

217. Should factors be unpredictable over time?

218. Is staff trained on the software technologies that are being used on the Integrated Architecture Framework project?

219. Has the approach and development strategy of the Integrated Architecture Framework project been defined, documented and accepted by the appropriate stakeholders?

220. Does the Integrated Architecture Framework project have a formal Integrated Architecture Framework project Plan?

221. What worked well?

2.8 Work Breakdown Structure: Integrated Architecture Framework

222. When do you stop?

223. Is it still viable?

224. How many levels?

225. Why would you develop a Work Breakdown Structure?

226. How much detail?

227. How big is a work-package?

228. Where does it take place?

229. What is the probability that the Integrated Architecture Framework project duration will exceed xx weeks?

230. Do you need another level?

231. When would you develop a Work Breakdown Structure?

232. How will you and your Integrated Architecture Framework project team define the Integrated Architecture Framework projects scope and work breakdown structure?

233. How far down?

234. Who has to do it?

235. Can you make it?

236. When does it have to be done?

237. Why is it useful?

238. What has to be done?

2.9 WBS Dictionary: Integrated Architecture Framework

239. The already stated responsible for overhead performance control of related costs?

240. The anticipated business volume?

241. Appropriate work authorization documents which subdivide the contractual effort and responsibilities, within functional organizations?

242. Is each control account assigned to a single organizational element directly responsible for the work and identifiable to a single element of the CWBS?

243. Budgets assigned to major functional organizations?

244. Are all elements of indirect expense identified to overhead cost budgets of Integrated Architecture Framework projections?

245. Is the anticipated (firm and potential) business base Integrated Architecture Framework projected in a rational, consistent manner?

246. Are all authorized tasks assigned to identified organizational elements?

247. Are estimates developed by Integrated Architecture Framework project personnel

coordinated with the already stated responsible for overall management to determine whether required resources will be available according to revised planning?

248. Are management actions taken to reduce indirect costs when there are significant adverse variances?

249. Is all budget available as management reserve identified and excluded from the performance measurement baseline?

250. Software specification, development, integration, and testing, licenses ?

251. Knowledgeable Integrated Architecture Framework projections of future performance?

252. Does the contractors system provide for the determination of cost variances attributable to the excess usage of material?

253. Can the contractor substantiate work package and planning package budgets?

254. What is the end result of a work package?

255. Intermediate schedules, as required, which provide a logical sequence from the master schedule to the control account level?

256. Does the contractor require sufficient detailed planning of control accounts to constrain the application of budget initially allocated for future effort to current effort?

257. Detailed schedules which support control account and work package start and completion dates/events?

2.10 Schedule Management Plan: Integrated Architecture Framework

258. Are Integrated Architecture Framework project contact logs kept up to date?

259. Will rolling way planning be used?

260. Have the procedures for identifying budget variances been followed?

261. Is there an onboarding process in place?

262. What will be the final cost of the Integrated Architecture Framework project if status quo is maintained?

263. Is a pmo (Integrated Architecture Framework project management office) in place and provide oversight to the Integrated Architecture Framework project?

264. Will the Integrated Architecture Framework project sponsor be involved in preliminary schedule reviews?

265. What does a valid Schedule look like?

266. What happens if a warning is triggered?

267. Have the key functions and capabilities been defined and assigned to each release or iteration?

268. Are Integrated Architecture Framework project leaders committed to this Integrated Architecture Framework project full time?

269. Are enough systems & user personnel assigned to the Integrated Architecture Framework project?

270. Are the processes for status updates and maintenance defined?

271. Pareto diagrams, statistical sampling, flow charting or trend analysis used quality monitoring?

272. Is there an excessive and invalid use of task constraints and relationships of leads/lags?

273. Is current scope of the Integrated Architecture Framework project substantially different than that originally defined?

274. Is your organization certified as a broker of the products/supplies?

275. Are all payments made according to the contract(s)?

276. Are the activity durations realistic and at an appropriate level of detail for effective management?

2.11 Activity List: Integrated Architecture Framework

277. How do you determine the late start (LS) for each activity?

278. How detailed should a Integrated Architecture Framework project get?

279. What will be performed?

280. For other activities, how much delay can be tolerated?

281. How difficult will it be to do specific activities on this Integrated Architecture Framework project?

282. What went right?

283. How should ongoing costs be monitored to try to keep the Integrated Architecture Framework project within budget?

284. How can the Integrated Architecture Framework project be displayed graphically to better visualize the activities?

285. Who will perform the work?

286. What went well?

287. Are the required resources available or need to be acquired?

288. What is the probability the Integrated Architecture Framework project can be completed in xx weeks?

289. When will the work be performed?

290. Is infrastructure setup part of your Integrated Architecture Framework project?

291. What is the LF and LS for each activity?

292. Can you determine the activity that must finish, before this activity can start?

293. How much slack is available in the Integrated Architecture Framework project?

294. In what sequence?

295. The wbs is developed as part of a joint planning session. and how do you know that youhave done this right?

2.12 Activity Attributes: Integrated Architecture Framework

296. What is missing?

297. Time for overtime?

298. How much activity detail is required?

299. How do you manage time?

300. How many days do you need to complete the work scope with a limit of X number of resources?

301. Activity: fair or not fair?

302. Where else does it apply?

303. Why?

304. Are the required resources available?

305. How difficult will it be to do specific activities on this Integrated Architecture Framework project?

306. Does your organization of the data change its meaning?

307. Can you re-assign any activities to another resource to resolve an over-allocation?

308. Do you feel very comfortable with your prediction?

309. What is your organizations history in doing similar activities?

310. Have you identified the Activity Leveling Priority code value on each activity?

311. Activity: what is Missing?

312. What is the general pattern here?

313. What activity do you think you should spend the most time on?

314. Would you consider either of corresponding activities an outlier?

2.13 Milestone List: Integrated Architecture Framework

315. Which path is the critical path?

316. How soon can the activity finish?

317. Competitive advantages?

318. Sustainable financial backing?

319. Level of the Innovation?

320. How late can each activity be finished and started?

321. How late can the activity finish?

322. Describe your organizations strengths and core competencies. What factors will make your organization succeed?

323. It is to be a narrative text providing the crucial aspects of your Integrated Architecture Framework project proposal answering what, who, how, when and where?

324. Who will manage the Integrated Architecture Framework project on a day-to-day basis?

325. Own known vulnerabilities?

326. Sustaining internal capabilities?

327. Identify critical paths (one or more) and which activities are on the critical path?

328. When will the Integrated Architecture Framework project be complete?

329. Calculate how long can activity be delayed?

330. Global influences?

331. New USPs?

2.14 Network Diagram: Integrated Architecture Framework

332. Planning: who, how long, what to do?

333. Exercise: what is the probability that the Integrated Architecture Framework project duration will exceed xx weeks?

334. What to do and When?

335. What job or jobs could run concurrently?

336. Which type of network diagram allows you to depict four types of dependencies?

337. What can be done concurrently?

338. What are the Major Administrative Issues?

339. Will crashing x weeks return more in benefits than it costs?

340. If a current contract exists, can you provide the vendor name, contract start, and contract expiration date?

341. What is the probability of completing the Integrated Architecture Framework project in less that xx days?

342. What activity must be completed immediately before this activity can start?

343. What controls the start and finish of a job?

344. Where do you schedule uncertainty time?

345. What is the lowest cost to complete this Integrated Architecture Framework project in xx weeks?

346. What job or jobs precede it?

347. Can you calculate the confidence level?

348. What is the completion time?

349. Where do schedules come from?

350. Are you on time?

2.15 Activity Resource Requirements: Integrated Architecture Framework

351. Why do you do that?

352. Which logical relationship does the PDM use most often?

353. When does monitoring begin?

354. How do you handle petty cash?

355. How many signatures do you require on a check and does this match what is in your policy and procedures?

356. Do you use tools like decomposition and rolling-wave planning to produce the activity list and other outputs?

357. Anything else?

358. Are there unresolved issues that need to be addressed?

359. Other support in specific areas?

360. What is the Work Plan Standard?

361. Organizational Applicability?

362. What are constraints that you might find during the Human Resource Planning process?

363. Is there anything planned that does not need to be here?

2.16 Resource Breakdown Structure: Integrated Architecture Framework

364. Which resource planning tool provides information on resource responsibility and accountability?

365. Any changes from stakeholders?

366. What are the requirements for resource data?

367. When do they need the information?

368. Why is this important?

369. Who will be used as a Integrated Architecture Framework project team member?

370. How can this help you with team building?

371. What is each stakeholders desired outcome for the Integrated Architecture Framework project?

372. What is the difference between % Complete and % work?

373. What is the number one predictor of a groups productivity?

374. Who is allowed to see what data about which resources?

375. What is Integrated Architecture Framework

project communication management?

376. Why time management?

377. What defines a successful Integrated Architecture Framework project?

378. Why do you do it?

379. Who is allowed to perform which functions?

380. What is the purpose of assigning and documenting responsibility?

2.17 Activity Duration Estimates: Integrated Architecture Framework

381. How can software assist in procuring goods and services?

382. What tasks can take place concurrently?

383. Have most organizations benefited from outsourcing?

384. Account for the make-or-buy process and how to perform the financial calculations involved in the process. What are the main types of contracts if you do decide to outsource?

385. How is the Integrated Architecture Framework project doing?

386. How can organizations use a weighted decision matrix to evaluate proposals as part of source selection?

387. Why is it important to determine activity sequencing on Integrated Architecture Framework projects?

388. How does the job market and current state of the economy affect human resource management?

389. What is the duration of the critical path for this Integrated Architecture Framework project?

390. What are some general rules of thumb for deciding if cost variance, schedule variance, cost performance index, and schedule performance index numbers are good or bad?

391. What are crucial elements of successful Integrated Architecture Framework project plan execution?

392. When a risk event occurs, is the risk response evaluated and the appropriate response implemented?

393. What are the main processes included in Integrated Architecture Framework project quality management?

394. Are expert judgment and historical information utilized to estimate activity duration?

395. How does a Integrated Architecture Framework project life cycle differ from a product life cycle?

396. Is the work performed reviewed against contractual objectives?

397. What are the ways to create and distribute Integrated Architecture Framework project performance information?

398. What are the typical challenges Integrated Architecture Framework project teams face during each of the five process groups?

2.18 Duration Estimating Worksheet: Integrated Architecture Framework

399. Define the work as completely as possible. What work will be included in the Integrated Architecture Framework project?

400. Is the Integrated Architecture Framework project responsive to community need?

401. What are the critical bottleneck activities?

402. Can the Integrated Architecture Framework project be constructed as planned?

403. Is this operation cost effective?

404. What is next?

405. Why estimate costs?

406. Done before proceeding with this activity or what can be done concurrently?

407. Value pocket identification & quantification what are value pockets?

408. What info is needed?

409. What is an Average Integrated Architecture Framework project?

410. When do the individual activities need to start

and finish?

411. Science = process: remember the scientific method?

412. What utility impacts are there?

413. Is a construction detail attached (to aid in explanation)?

414. What questions do you have?

2.19 Project Schedule: Integrated Architecture Framework

415. What are you counting on?

416. Verify that the update is accurate. Are all remaining durations correct?

417. Is the Integrated Architecture Framework project schedule available for all Integrated Architecture Framework project team members to review?

418. Why do you need to manage Integrated Architecture Framework project Risk?

419. How detailed should a Integrated Architecture Framework project get?

420. Is infrastructure setup part of your Integrated Architecture Framework project?

421. To what degree is do you feel the entire team was committed to the Integrated Architecture Framework project schedule?

422. Month Integrated Architecture Framework project take?

423. How do you use schedules?

424. Why is this particularly bad?

425. Are procedures defined by which the Integrated

Architecture Framework project schedule may be changed?

426. Are you working on the right risks?

427. Is there a Schedule Management Plan that establishes the criteria and activities for developing, monitoring and controlling the Integrated Architecture Framework project schedule?

428. Are the original Integrated Architecture Framework project schedule and budget realistic?

429. Schedule/cost recovery?

430. Your Integrated Architecture Framework project management plan results in a Integrated Architecture Framework project schedule that is too long. If the Integrated Architecture Framework project network diagram cannot change and you have extra personnel resources, what is the BEST thing to do?

431. Integrated Architecture Framework project work estimates Who is managing the work estimate quality of work tasks in the Integrated Architecture Framework project schedule?

432. What is Integrated Architecture Framework project management?

2.20 Cost Management Plan: Integrated Architecture Framework

433. What does this mean to a cost or scheduler manager?

434. Cost tracking and performance analysis – How will cost tracking and performance analysis be accomplished?

435. Does the resource management plan include a personnel development plan?

436. Is the Integrated Architecture Framework project sponsor clearly communicating the business case or rationale for why this Integrated Architecture Framework project is needed?

437. Are trade-offs between accepting the risk and mitigating the risk identified?

438. Forecasts – how will the cost to complete the Integrated Architecture Framework project be forecast?

439. Is the Integrated Architecture Framework project schedule available for all Integrated Architecture Framework project team members to review?

440. Scope of work – What is the likelihood and extent of potential future changes to the Integrated Architecture Framework project scope?

441. Has a sponsor been identified?

442. Mitigation – based on the action, cost and probability of success, will the mitigation be made?

443. Are all resource assumptions documented?

444. Do Integrated Architecture Framework project managers participating in the Integrated Architecture Framework project know the Integrated Architecture Framework projects true status first hand?

445. Are the quality tools and methods identified in the Quality Plan appropriate to the Integrated Architecture Framework project?

446. Owner, contractor, and subcontractors?

447. Vac -variance at completion, how much over/ under budget do you expect to be?

448. Integrated Architecture Framework project Objectives?

449. Schedule contingency – how will the schedule contingency be administrated?

450. Are Integrated Architecture Framework project leaders committed to this Integrated Architecture Framework project full time?

2.21 Activity Cost Estimates: Integrated Architecture Framework

451. Specific - is the objective clear in terms of what, how, when, and where the situation will be changed?

452. What is the Integrated Architecture Framework projects sustainability strategy that will ensure Integrated Architecture Framework project results will endure or be sustained?

453. One way to define activities is to consider how organization employees describe jobs to families and friends. You basically want to know, What do you do?

454. Does the activity serve a common type of customer?

455. What is a Integrated Architecture Framework project Management Plan?

456. Where can you get activity reports?

457. How do you change activities?

458. Eac -estimate at completion, what is the total job expected to cost?

459. How and when do you enter into Integrated Architecture Framework project Procurement Management?

460. What are the audit requirements?

461. Can you delete activities or make them inactive?

462. Was it performed on time?

463. How do you treat administrative costs in the activity inventory?

464. Performance bond should always provide what part of the contract value?

465. If you are asked to lower your estimate because the price is too high, what are your options?

466. Were you satisfied with the work?

467. What skill level is required to do the job?

468. How Award?

2.22 Cost Estimating Worksheet: Integrated Architecture Framework

469. Who is best positioned to know and assist in identifying corresponding factors?

470. What is the estimated labor cost today based upon this information?

471. Is the Integrated Architecture Framework project responsive to community need?

472. What additional Integrated Architecture Framework project(s) could be initiated as a result of this Integrated Architecture Framework project?

473. How will the results be shared and to whom?

474. Ask: are others positioned to know, are others credible, and will others cooperate?

475. What will others want?

476. What happens to any remaining funds not used?

477. What costs are to be estimated?

478. Will the Integrated Architecture Framework project collaborate with the local community and leverage resources?

479. Does the Integrated Architecture Framework project provide innovative ways for stakeholders to

overcome obstacles or deliver better outcomes?

480. What can be included?

481. Identify the timeframe necessary to monitor progress and collect data to determine how the selected measure has changed?

482. Is it feasible to establish a control group arrangement?

483. Can a trend be established from historical performance data on the selected measure and are the criteria for using trend analysis or forecasting methods met?

484. What is the purpose of estimating?

2.23 Cost Baseline: Integrated Architecture Framework

485. If you sold 10x widgets on a day, what would the affect on profits be?

486. Have the lessons learned been filed with the Integrated Architecture Framework project Management Office?

487. On budget?

488. Have all the product or service deliverables been accepted by the customer?

489. Impact to environment?

490. Are there contingencies or conditions related to the acceptance?

491. Has training and knowledge transfer of the operations organization been completed?

492. Has the Integrated Architecture Framework projected annual cost to operate and maintain the product(s) or service(s) been approved and funded?

493. How fast?

494. Pcs for your new business. what would the life cycle costs be?

495. Does the suggested change request seem to

represent a necessary enhancement to the product?

496. Are you asking management for something as a result of this update?

497. How long are you willing to wait before you find out were late?

498. Verify business objectives. Are others appropriate, and well-articulated?

499. Is the cr within Integrated Architecture Framework project scope?

500. Should a more thorough impact analysis be conducted?

501. Have you identified skills that are missing from your team?

2.24 Quality Management Plan: Integrated Architecture Framework

502. How is equipment calibrated?

503. How are calibration records kept?

504. After observing execution of process, is it in compliance with the documented Plan?

505. What are the appropriate test methods to be used?

506. Were there any deficiencies / issues identified in the prior years self-assessment?

507. Do you keep back-up copies of any data?

508. List your organizations customer contact standards that employees are expected to maintain. How are corresponding standards measured?

509. Is this process still needed?

510. Why quality management?

511. How is staff informed of proper reporting methods?

512. Where do you focus?

513. How does your organization measure customer satisfaction/dissatisfaction?

514. Has a Integrated Architecture Framework project Communications Plan been developed?

515. What is quality and how will you ensure it?

516. Are there unnecessary steps that are creating bottlenecks and/or causing people to wait?

517. Are there standards for code development?

518. With the five whys method, the team considers why the issue being explored occurred. do others then take that initial answer and ask why?

2.25 Quality Metrics: Integrated Architecture Framework

519. Was review conducted per standard protocols?

520. Should a modifier be included?

521. Does risk analysis documentation meet standards?

522. What metrics are important and most beneficial to measure?

523. How do you know if everyone is trying to improve the right things?

524. How are requirements conflicts resolved?

525. Where is quality now?

526. What are your organizations next steps?

527. Are there any open risk issues?

528. Has it met internal or external standards?

529. How do you measure?

530. Are quality metrics defined?

531. What percentage are outcome-based?

532. How should customers provide input?

533. Can you correlate your quality metrics to profitability?

534. Is material complete (and does it meet the standards)?

535. What if the biggest risk to your business were the already stated people who do not complain?

536. Which are the right metrics to use?

537. What can manufacturing professionals do to ensure quality is seen as an integral part of the entire product lifecycle?

538. Has trace of defects been initiated?

2.26 Process Improvement Plan: Integrated Architecture Framework

539. Have storage and access mechanisms and procedures been determined?

540. How do you manage quality?

541. If a process improvement framework is being used, which elements will help the problems and goals listed?

542. Does your process ensure quality?

543. What makes people good SPI coaches?

544. Are you making progress on the goals?

545. What personnel are the coaches for your initiative?

546. Modeling current processes is great, and will you ever see a return on that investment?

547. What personnel are the change agents for your initiative?

548. Are you making progress on your improvement plan?

549. Management commitment at all levels?

550. What is the test-cycle concept?

551. Has the time line required to move measurement results from the points of collection to databases or users been established?

552. The motive is determined by asking, Why do you want to achieve this goal?

553. Does explicit definition of the measures exist?

554. Where do you want to be?

555. What actions are needed to address the problems and achieve the goals?

2.27 Responsibility Assignment Matrix: Integrated Architecture Framework

556. Are material costs reported within the same period as that in which BCWP is earned for that material?

557. Competencies and craftsmanship – what competencies are necessary and what level?

558. The staff interests – is the group or the person interested in working for this Integrated Architecture Framework project?

559. What expertise is available in your department?

560. Does the contractors system include procedures for measuring the performance of critical subcontractors?

561. Too many is: do all the identified roles need to be routinely informed or only in exceptional circumstances?

562. Are overhead cost budgets established for each organization which has authority to incur overhead costs?

563. Not any rs, as, or cs: if an identified role is only informed, should others be eliminated from the matrix?

564. Ideas for developing soft skills at your organization?

565. Evaluate the impact of schedule changes, work around, etc?

566. Does the contractor use objective results, design reviews and tests to trace schedule performance?

567. How many hours by each staff member/rate?

568. Is the entire contract planned in time-phased control accounts to the extent practicable?

569. What can you do to improve productivity?

570. Budgets assigned to control accounts?

2.28 Roles and Responsibilities: Integrated Architecture Framework

571. Does the team have access to and ability to use data analysis tools?

572. What areas would you highlight for changes or improvements?

573. What is working well?

574. How well did the Integrated Architecture Framework project Team understand the expectations of specific roles and responsibilities?

575. What are your major roles and responsibilities in the area of performance measurement and assessment?

576. What specific behaviors did you observe?

577. Concern: where are you limited or have no authority, where you can not influence?

578. How is your work-life balance?

579. Key conclusions and recommendations: Are conclusions and recommendations relevant and acceptable?

580. What areas of supervision are challenging for you?

581. Are governance roles and responsibilities documented?

582. Do the values and practices inherent in the culture of your organization foster or hinder the process?

583. Influence: what areas of organizational decision making are you able to influence when you do not have authority to make the final decision?

584. What should you do now to ensure that you are meeting all expectations of your current position?

585. Are your budgets supportive of a culture of quality data?

586. Once the responsibilities are defined for the Integrated Architecture Framework project, have the deliverables, roles and responsibilities been clearly communicated to every participant?

587. What should you highlight for improvement?

588. What is working well within your organizations performance management system?

589. Be specific; avoid generalities. Thank you and great work alone are insufficient. What exactly do you appreciate and why?

2.29 Human Resource Management Plan: Integrated Architecture Framework

590. Is the Integrated Architecture Framework project schedule available for all Integrated Architecture Framework project team members to review?

591. Identify who is needed on the core Integrated Architecture Framework project team to complete Integrated Architecture Framework project deliverables and achieve its goals and objectives. What skills, knowledge and experiences are required?

592. Was your organizations estimating methodology being used and followed?

593. Is this Integrated Architecture Framework project carried out in partnership with other groups/ organizations?

594. Does the Integrated Architecture Framework project have a Statement of Work?

595. Are there checklists created to determine if all quality processes are followed?

596. Are action items captured and managed?

597. Have all involved Integrated Architecture Framework project stakeholders and work groups committed to the Integrated Architecture Framework project?

598. Does the business case include how the Integrated Architecture Framework project aligns with your organizations strategic goals & objectives?

599. Were Integrated Architecture Framework project team members involved in the development of activity & task decomposition?

600. Have reserves been created to address risks?

601. Is the current culture aligned with the vision, mission, and values of the department?

602. Is there a set of procedures defining the scope, procedures, and deliverables defining quality control?

603. Has a provision been made to reassess Integrated Architecture Framework project risks at various Integrated Architecture Framework project stages?

604. Are enough systems & user personnel assigned to the Integrated Architecture Framework project?

605. Has the budget been baselined?

2.30 Communications Management Plan: Integrated Architecture Framework

606. What steps can you take for a positive relationship?

607. Are the stakeholders getting the information others need, are others consulted, are concerns addressed?

608. Who have you worked with in past, similar initiatives?

609. Who is the stakeholder?

610. Which stakeholders are thought leaders, influences, or early adopters?

611. Do you prepare stakeholder engagement plans?

612. Do you feel a register helps?

613. How did the term stakeholder originate?

614. Is the stakeholder role recognized by your organization?

615. Will messages be directly related to the release strategy or phases of the Integrated Architecture Framework project?

616. Who is responsible?

617. Who did you turn to if you had questions?

618. Who to share with?

619. Do you ask; can you recommend others for you to talk with about this initiative?

620. What to know?

621. Conflict resolution -which method when?

622. How often do you engage with stakeholders?

623. How is this initiative related to other portfolios, programs, or Integrated Architecture Framework projects?

624. How do you manage communications?

2.31 Risk Management Plan: Integrated Architecture Framework

625. Do you have a consistent repeatable process that is actually used?

626. What other risks are created by choosing an avoidance strategy?

627. Technology risk: is the Integrated Architecture Framework project technically feasible?

628. What will drive change?

629. Are there alternative opinions/solutions/ processes you should explore?

630. Are certain activities taking a long time to complete?

631. How risk averse are you?

632. If you can not fix it, how do you do it differently?

633. Can the risk be avoided by choosing a different alternative?

634. Can you stabilize dynamic risk factors?

635. Are tool mentors available?

636. Are enough people available?

637. Is the customer willing to participate in reviews?

638. For software; are compilers and code generators available and suitable for the product to be built?

639. Is there anything you would now do differently on your Integrated Architecture Framework project based on this experience?

640. Are the required plans included, such as nonstructural flood risk management plans?

641. Are the metrics meaningful and useful?

642. What are the cost, schedule and resource impacts if the risk does occur?

643. Should the risk be taken at all?

644. Do the people have the right combinations of skills?

2.32 Risk Register: Integrated Architecture Framework

645. What may happen or not go according to plan?

646. Budget and schedule: what are the estimated costs and schedules for performing risk-related activities?

647. Are implemented controls working as others should?

648. What can be done about it?

649. Are there any knock-on effects/impact on any of the other areas?

650. How could corresponding Risk affect the Integrated Architecture Framework project in terms of cost and schedule?

651. What are the major risks facing the Integrated Architecture Framework project?

652. People risk -are people with appropriate skills available to help complete the Integrated Architecture Framework project?

653. What is your current and future risk profile?

654. What are you going to do to limit the Integrated Architecture Framework projects risk exposure due to the identified risks?

655. When will it happen?

656. What risks might negatively or positively affect achieving the Integrated Architecture Framework project objectives?

657. Assume the event happens, what is the Most Likely impact?

658. What would the impact to the Integrated Architecture Framework project objectives be should the risk arise?

659. What is the reason for current performance gaps and do the risks and opportunities identified previously account for this?

660. How is a Community Risk Register created?

661. Having taken action, how did the responses effect change, and where is the Integrated Architecture Framework project now?

662. What is a Community Risk Register?

2.33 Probability and Impact Assessment: Integrated Architecture Framework

663. How would you assess the risk management process in the Integrated Architecture Framework project?

664. Are Integrated Architecture Framework project requirements stable?

665. Has something like this been done before?

666. Are end-users enthusiastically committed to the Integrated Architecture Framework project and the system/product to be built?

667. How much risk do others need to take?

668. Is a software Integrated Architecture Framework project management tool available?

669. Management -what contingency plans do you have if the risk becomes a reality?

670. Does the Integrated Architecture Framework project team have experience with the technology to be implemented?

671. Will new information become available during the Integrated Architecture Framework project?

672. What new technologies are being explored in the

same area?

673. How are the local factors going to affect the absorption?

674. Who should be responsible for the monitoring and tracking of the indicators youhave identified?

675. Monitoring of the overall Integrated Architecture Framework project status – are there any changes in the Integrated Architecture Framework project that can effect and cause new possible risks?

676. What can you do to minimize the impact if it does?

677. What are the tools and techniques used in managing the challenges faced?

678. Is the customer willing to establish rapid communication links with the developer?

679. What are its business ethics?

680. Are the risk data complete?

681. Is the number of people on the Integrated Architecture Framework project team adequate to do the job?

2.34 Probability and Impact Matrix: Integrated Architecture Framework

682. During Integrated Architecture Framework project executing, a team member identifies a risk that is not in the risk register. What should you do?

683. What would you do differently?

684. What kind of preparation would be required to do this?

685. What should be done with non-critical risks?

686. Who has experience with this?

687. Economic to take on the Integrated Architecture Framework project?

688. Which of the risk factors can be avoided altogether?

689. How solid are the price-volume Integrated Architecture Framework projections?

690. Are people attending meetings and doing work?

691. What is the level of commitment and professionalism?

692. Premium on reliability of product?

693. What action do you usually take against risks?

694. What should be done with risks on the watch list?

695. What things might go wrong?

696. Are the risk data timely and relevant?

697. Have staff received necessary training?

698. What action would you take to the identified risks in the Integrated Architecture Framework project?

699. Number of users of the product?

700. Will there be an increase in the political conservatism?

2.35 Risk Data Sheet: Integrated Architecture Framework

701. Who has a vested interest in how you perform as your organization (our stakeholders)?

702. What are you trying to achieve (Objectives)?

703. What if client refuses?

704. What actions can be taken to eliminate or remove risk?

705. Do effective diagnostic tests exist?

706. What are your core values?

707. Potential for recurrence?

708. What are you weak at and therefore need to do better?

709. Is the data sufficiently specified in terms of the type of failure being analyzed, and its frequency or probability?

710. What are you here for (Mission)?

711. What do people affected think about the need for, and practicality of preventive measures?

712. How do you handle product safely?

713. Type of risk identified?

714. How can it happen?

715. Has a sensitivity analysis been carried out?

716. What was measured?

717. Whom do you serve (customers)?

718. Will revised controls lead to tolerable risk levels?

719. Has the most cost-effective solution been chosen?

2.36 Procurement Management Plan: Integrated Architecture Framework

720. Are Integrated Architecture Framework project team members committed fulltime?

721. Are status reports received per the Integrated Architecture Framework project Plan?

722. Are key risk mitigation strategies added to the Integrated Architecture Framework project schedule?

723. Are Integrated Architecture Framework project contact logs kept up to date?

724. Are actuals compared against estimates to analyze and correct variances?

725. Is the current scope of the Integrated Architecture Framework project substantially different than that originally defined?

726. Public engagement – did you get it right?

727. Based on your Integrated Architecture Framework project communication management plan, what worked well?

728. Sensitivity analysis?

729. How will the duration of the Integrated Architecture Framework project influence your decisions?

730. Is the quality assurance team identified?

731. Do you have the reasons why the changes to your organizational systems and capabilities are required?

732. Does the Integrated Architecture Framework project have a Statement of Work?

733. If standardized procurement documents are needed, where can others be found?

2.37 Source Selection Criteria: Integrated Architecture Framework

734. Can you make a cost/technical tradeoff?

735. When should debriefings be held and how should they be scheduled?

736. What are the special considerations for preaward debriefings?

737. Are considerations anticipated?

738. Does the evaluation of any change include an impact analysis; how will the change affect the scope, time, cost, and quality of the goods or services being provided?

739. Can you reasonably estimate total organization requirements for the coming year?

740. What are the requirements for publicizing a RFP?

741. What information may not be provided?

742. Can you prevent comparison of proposals?

743. Do you have a plan to document consensus results including disposition of any disagreement by individual evaluators?

744. How do you encourage efficiency and consistency?

745. What procedures are followed when a contractor requires access to classified information or a significant quantity of special material/information?

746. In order of importance, which evaluation criteria are the most critical to the determination of your overall rating?

747. What are the guiding principles for developing an evaluation report?

748. Do proposed hours support content and schedule?

749. Are there any specific considerations that precludes offers from being selected as the awardee?

750. How should the preproposal conference be conducted?

751. How do you manage procurement?

752. Who should attend debriefings?

753. Is experience evaluated?

2.38 Stakeholder Management Plan: Integrated Architecture Framework

754. Has a provision been made to reassess Integrated Architecture Framework project risks at various Integrated Architecture Framework project stages?

755. Were the budget estimates reasonable?

756. How will the equipment be verified?

757. Is there an issues management plan in place?

758. How is information analyzed, and what specific pieces of data would be of interest to the Integrated Architecture Framework project manager?

759. Why would a customer be interested in a particular product or service?

760. Is the amount of effort justified by the anticipated value of forming a new process?

761. Are post milestone Integrated Architecture Framework project reviews (PMPR) conducted with your organization at least once a year?

762. Does the plan conform to standards?

763. Are assumptions being identified, recorded, analyzed, qualified and closed?

764. What records are required (eg purchase orders,

agreements)?

765. Has the Integrated Architecture Framework project manager been identified?

766. Are vendor invoices audited for accuracy before payment?

767. Have all stakeholders been identified?

768. Are parking lot items captured?

769. What is the difference between product and Integrated Architecture Framework project scope?

2.39 Change Management Plan: Integrated Architecture Framework

770. Has the relevant business unit been notified of installation and support requirements?

771. Is there an adequate supply of people for the new roles?

772. Readiness -what is a successful end state?

773. Who might be able to help you the most?

774. What time commitment will this involve?

775. How will the stakeholders share information and transfer knowledge?

776. What are you trying to achieve as a result of communication?

777. Is there support for this application(s) and are the details available for distribution?

778. What skills, education, knowledge, or work experiences should the resources have for each identified competency?

779. What policies and procedures need to be changed?

780. Do there need to be new channels developed?

781. Impact of systems implementation on organization change?

782. What are the major changes to processes?

783. Who might present the most resistance?

784. What does a resilient organization look like?

785. What are the needs, priorities and special interests of the audience?

786. When does it make sense to customize?

787. What are the training strategies?

788. What provokes organizational change?

3.0 Executing Process Group: Integrated Architecture Framework

789. How well did the chosen processes produce the expected results?

790. Were sponsors and decision makers available when needed outside regularly scheduled meetings?

791. How many different communication channels does the Integrated Architecture Framework project team have?

792. What are the main types of goods and services being outsourced?

793. What good practices or successful experiences or transferable examples have been identified?

794. What type of people would you want on your team?

795. Would you rate yourself as being risk-averse, risk-neutral, or risk-seeking?

796. Based on your Integrated Architecture Framework project communication management plan, what worked well?

797. What are the main parts of the scope statement?

798. What are the challenges Integrated Architecture Framework project teams face?

799. What are the key components of the Integrated Architecture Framework project communications plan?

800. What are the typical Integrated Architecture Framework project management skills?

801. On which process should team members spend the most time?

802. What factors are contributing to progress or delay in the achievement of products and results?

803. How can you use Microsoft Integrated Architecture Framework project and Excel to assist in Integrated Architecture Framework project risk management?

804. When is the appropriate time to bring the scorecard to Board meetings?

805. When will the Integrated Architecture Framework project be done?

3.1 Team Member Status Report: Integrated Architecture Framework

806. How much risk is involved?

807. The problem with Reward & Recognition Programs is that the truly deserving people all too often get left out. How can you make it practical?

808. How it is to be done?

809. Is there evidence that staff is taking a more professional approach toward management of your organizations Integrated Architecture Framework projects?

810. Why is it to be done?

811. When a teams productivity and success depend on collaboration and the efficient flow of information, what generally fails them?

812. How can you make it practical?

813. How will resource planning be done?

814. Are the products of your organizations Integrated Architecture Framework projects meeting customers objectives?

815. What is to be done?

816. Will the staff do training or is that done by a third

party?

817. What specific interest groups do you have in place?

818. Does your organization have the means (staff, money, contract, etc.) to produce or to acquire the product, good, or service?

819. Are your organizations Integrated Architecture Framework projects more successful over time?

820. Do you have an Enterprise Integrated Architecture Framework project Management Office (EPMO)?

821. How does this product, good, or service meet the needs of the Integrated Architecture Framework project and your organization as a whole?

822. Does the product, good, or service already exist within your organization?

823. Are the attitudes of staff regarding Integrated Architecture Framework project work improving?

824. Does every department have to have a Integrated Architecture Framework project Manager on staff?

3.2 Change Request: Integrated Architecture Framework

825. How shall the implementation of changes be recorded?

826. What are the basic mechanics of the Change Advisory Board (CAB)?

827. Who is responsible to authorize changes?

828. How does a team identify the discrete elements of a configuration?

829. Will this change conflict with other requirements changes (e.g., lead to conflicting operational scenarios)?

830. Is it feasible to use requirements attributes as predictors of reliability?

831. Customer acceptance plan how will the customer verify the change has been implemented successfully?

832. Has a formal technical review been conducted to assess technical correctness?

833. How does your organization control changes before and after software is released to a customer?

834. Screen shots or attachments included in a Change Request?

835. What needs to be communicated?

836. What has an inspector to inspect and to check?

837. Change request coordination ?

838. Does the schedule include Integrated Architecture Framework project management time and change request analysis time?

839. Who is included in the change control team?

840. Will all change requests and current status be logged?

841. What can be filed?

842. Are there requirements attributes that are strongly related to the complexity and size?

843. Will all change requests be unconditionally tracked through this process?

844. When to submit a change request?

3.3 Change Log: Integrated Architecture Framework

845. Is this a mandatory replacement?

846. When was the request submitted?

847. Do the described changes impact on the integrity or security of the system?

848. Is the requested change request a result of changes in other Integrated Architecture Framework project(s)?

849. Is the change request within Integrated Architecture Framework project scope?

850. Does the suggested change request represent a desired enhancement to the products functionality?

851. Where do changes come from?

852. How does this change affect the timeline of the schedule?

853. How does this change affect scope?

854. Who initiated the change request?

855. Is the change backward compatible without limitations?

856. When was the request approved?

857. How does this relate to the standards developed for specific business processes?

858. Is the change request open, closed or pending?

859. Will the Integrated Architecture Framework project fail if the change request is not executed?

860. Is the submitted change a new change or a modification of a previously approved change?

3.4 Decision Log: Integrated Architecture Framework

861. How do you know when you are achieving it?

862. Adversarial environment. is your opponent open to a non-traditional workflow, or will it likely challenge anything you do?

863. Linked to original objective?

864. How effective is maintaining the log at facilitating organizational learning?

865. What is the average size of your matters in an applicable measurement?

866. What is the line where eDiscovery ends and document review begins?

867. How does provision of information, both in terms of content and presentation, influence acceptance of alternative strategies?

868. Who will be given a copy of this document and where will it be kept?

869. What is your overall strategy for quality control / quality assurance procedures?

870. Is your opponent open to a non-traditional workflow, or will it likely challenge anything you do?

871. Does anything need to be adjusted?

872. What eDiscovery problem or issue did your organization set out to fix or make better?

873. Decision-making process; how will the team make decisions?

874. Which variables make a critical difference?

875. How do you define success?

876. What was the rationale for the decision?

877. Do strategies and tactics aimed at less than full control reduce the costs of management or simply shift the cost burden?

878. Who is the decisionmaker?

879. At what point in time does loss become unacceptable?

880. What alternatives/risks were considered?

3.5 Quality Audit: Integrated Architecture Framework

881. How does your organization know that the range and quality of its social and recreational services and facilities are appropriately effective and constructive in meeting the needs of staff?

882. Are all records associated with the reconditioning of a device maintained for a minimum of two years after the sale or disposal of the last device within a lot of merchandise?

883. Is there a written corporate quality policy?

884. How does your organization know that its Governance system is appropriately effective and constructive?

885. How does your organization know that its information technology system is serving its needs as effectively and constructively as is appropriate?

886. Does the audit organization have experience in performing the required work for entities of your type and size?

887. How does your organization know that its promotions system is appropriately effective, constructive and fair?

888. Are complaint files maintained?

889. How are you auditing your organizations compliance with regulations?

890. How does your organization know that its system for recruiting the best staff possible are appropriately effective and constructive?

891. How do staff know if they are doing a good job?

892. How does your organization know that its system for commercializing research outputs is appropriately effective and constructive?

893. What are your supplier audits?

894. Are there appropriate indicators for monitoring the effectiveness and efficiency of processes?

895. Can your organization demonstrate exactly how and why results were achieved?

896. What is your organizations greatest strength?

897. How does your organization know that the support for its staff is appropriately effective and constructive?

898. What will the Observer get to Observe?

899. What happens if your organization fails its Quality Audit?

900. Are there sufficient personnel having the necessary education, background, training, and experience to assure that all operations are correctly performed?

3.6 Team Directory: Integrated Architecture Framework

901. Who should receive information (all stakeholders)?

902. Who will report Integrated Architecture Framework project status to all stakeholders?

903. Process decisions: do job conditions warrant additional actions to collect job information and document on-site activity?

904. Process decisions: which organizational elements and which individuals will be assigned management functions?

905. Process decisions: are there any statutory or regulatory issues relevant to the timely execution of work?

906. How will the team handle changes?

907. Process decisions: is work progressing on schedule and per contract requirements?

908. Is construction on schedule?

909. Process decisions: are contractors adequately prosecuting the work?

910. Process decisions: are all start-up, turn over and close out requirements of the contract satisfied?

911. Who will be the stakeholders on your next Integrated Architecture Framework project?

912. Contract requirements complied with?

913. How and in what format should information be presented?

914. How do unidentified risks impact the outcome of the Integrated Architecture Framework project?

915. How will you accomplish and manage the objectives?

916. Days from the time the issue is identified?

917. Who are the Team Members?

3.7 Team Operating Agreement: Integrated Architecture Framework

918. What are the boundaries (organizational or geographic) within which you operate?

919. What is culture?

920. Do you call or email participants to ensure understanding, follow-through and commitment to the meeting outcomes?

921. Reimbursements: how will the team members be reimbursed for expenses and time commitments?

922. Does your team need access to all documents and information at all times?

923. Have you established procedures that team members can follow to work effectively together, such as a team operating agreement?

924. Do you use a parking lot for any items that are important and outside of the agenda?

925. Do you upload presentation materials in advance and test the technology?

926. Do you determine the meeting length and time of day?

927. What types of accommodations will be formulated and put in place for sustaining the team?

928. Did you determine the technology methods that best match the messages to be communicated?

929. How will you resolve conflict efficiently and respectfully?

930. Seconds for members to respond?

931. Do team members reside in more than two countries?

932. What individual strengths does each team member bring to the group?

933. Communication protocols: how will the team communicate?

934. Did you recap the meeting purpose, time, and expectations?

935. To whom do you deliver your services?

936. Is compensation based on team and individual performance?

937. The method to be used in the decision making process; Will it be consensus, majority rule, or the supervisor having the final say?

3.8 Team Performance Assessment: Integrated Architecture Framework

938. To what degree do team members articulate the teams work approach?

939. To what degree will new and supplemental skills be introduced as the need is recognized?

940. Effects of crew composition on crew performance: Does the whole equal the sum of its parts?

941. Can team performance be reliably measured in simulator and live exercises using the same assessment tool?

942. To what degree will the approach capitalize on and enhance the skills of all team members in a manner that takes into consideration other demands on members of the team?

943. What is method variance?

944. To what degree does the teams work approach provide opportunity for members to engage in results-based evaluation?

945. Individual task proficiency and team process behavior: what is important for team functioning?

946. To what degree does the teams work approach provide opportunity for members to engage in open

interaction?

947. To what degree do team members feel that the purpose of the team is important, if not exciting?

948. To what degree can all members engage in open and interactive considerations?

949. Can familiarity breed backup?

950. Where to from here?

951. To what degree are the members clear on what they are individually responsible for and what they are jointly responsible for?

952. Do you give group members authority to make at least some important decisions?

953. To what degree are the relative importance and priority of the goals clear to all team members?

954. To what degree can the team measure progress against specific goals?

955. To what degree do the goals specify concrete team work products?

956. To what degree can team members meet frequently enough to accomplish the teams ends?

957. To what degree does the team possess adequate membership to achieve its ends?

3.9 Team Member Performance Assessment: Integrated Architecture Framework

958. Does adaptive training work?

959. What future plans (e.g., modifications) do you have for your program?

960. Goals met?

961. How is your organizations Strategic Management System tied to performance measurement?

962. What qualities does a successful Team leader possess?

963. How do you work together to improve teaching and learning?

964. What kinds of performance factors / elements do you use?

965. What evaluation results did you have?

966. What are acceptable governance changes?

967. To what degree do team members understand one anothers roles and skills?

968. How should adaptive assessments be implemented?

969. What makes them effective?

970. To what degree is there a sense that only the team can succeed?

971. What are they responsible for?

972. Does platform-specific assessment information contribute to training placement or tailoring of instruction (e.g. aptitude-treatment interaction)?

973. What evidence supports your decision-making?

974. Does the rater (supervisor) have to wait for the interim or final performance assessment review to tell an employee that the employees performance is unsatisfactory?

975. For what period of time is a member rated?

3.10 Issue Log: Integrated Architecture Framework

976. Can you think of other people who might have concerns or interests?

977. Can an impact cause deviation beyond team, stage or Integrated Architecture Framework project tolerances?

978. What does the stakeholder need from the team?

979. Who is involved as you identify stakeholders?

980. Do you often overlook a key stakeholder or stakeholder group?

981. Are the stakeholders getting the information they need, are they consulted, are concerns addressed?

982. Why multiple evaluators?

983. Are there common objectives between the team and the stakeholder?

984. Is access to the Issue Log controlled?

985. Why do you manage human resources?

986. Do you have members of your team responsible for certain stakeholders?

987. Where do team members get information?

988. What is the impact on the Business Case?

989. In your work, how much time is spent on stakeholder identification?

990. What is the status of the issue?

991. Who reported the issue?

992. What effort will a change need?

993. Who needs to know and how much?

994. Who are the members of the governing body?

4.0 Monitoring and Controlling Process Group: Integrated Architecture Framework

995. Who are the Integrated Architecture Framework project stakeholders?

996. What were things that you did very well and want to do the same again on the next Integrated Architecture Framework project?

997. How should needs be met?

998. Does the solution fit in with organizations technical architectural requirements?

999. Key stakeholders to work with. How many potential communications channels exist on the Integrated Architecture Framework project?

1000. If action is called for, what form should it take?

1001. When will the Integrated Architecture Framework project be done?

1002. Is there sufficient funding available for this?

1003. What are the deliverables?

1004. Where is the Risk in the Integrated Architecture Framework project?

1005. What do they need to know about the

Integrated Architecture Framework project?

1006. What areas does the group agree are the biggest success on the Integrated Architecture Framework project?

1007. What input will you be required to provide the Integrated Architecture Framework project team?

1008. Is there sufficient time allotted between the general system design and the detailed system design phases?

1009. Is progress on outcomes due to your program?

1010. How do you monitor progress?

1011. Were escalated issues resolved promptly?

1012. Change, where should you look for problems?

4.1 Project Performance Report: Integrated Architecture Framework

1013. To what degree do the structures of the formal organization motivate taskrelevant behavior and facilitate task completion?

1014. To what degree do all members feel responsible for all agreed-upon measures?

1015. To what degree does the task meet individual needs?

1016. To what degree does the teams approach to its work allow for modification and improvement over time?

1017. To what degree are the structures of the formal organization consistent with the behaviors in the informal organization?

1018. To what degree do the relationships of the informal organization motivate taskrelevant behavior and facilitate task completion?

1019. To what degree do members articulate the goals beyond the team membership?

1020. To what degree does the formal organization make use of individual resources and meet individual needs?

1021. To what degree does the teams work approach

provide opportunity for members to engage in fact-based problem solving?

1022. To what degree are the goals realistic?

1023. To what degree will team members, individually and collectively, commit time to help themselves and others learn and develop skills?

1024. To what degree are sub-teams possible or necessary?

1025. How is the data used?

1026. What is the degree to which rules govern information exchange between individuals within your organization?

1027. To what degree is the information network consistent with the structure of the formal organization?

4.2 Variance Analysis: Integrated Architecture Framework

1028. Contract line items and end items?

1029. How do you identify and isolate causes of favorable and unfavorable cost and schedule variances?

1030. What business event caused the fluctuation?

1031. What causes selling price variance?

1032. Favorable or unfavorable variance?

1033. How does the use of a single conversion element (rather than the traditional labor and overhead elements) affect standard costing?

1034. Is work properly classified as measured effort, LOE, or apportioned effort and appropriately separated?

1035. Are overhead cost budgets established for each department which has authority to incur overhead costs?

1036. Who are responsible for the establishment of budgets and assignment of resources for overhead performance?

1037. Are indirect costs charged to the appropriate indirect pools and incurring organization?

1038. Are records maintained to show how management reserves are used?

1039. Can process improvements lead to unfavorable variances?

1040. Is the anticipated (firm and potential) business base Integrated Architecture Framework projected in a rational, consistent manner?

1041. Is budgeted cost for work performed calculated in a manner consistent with the way work is planned?

1042. Who are responsible for overhead performance control of related costs?

1043. Does the contractors system identify work accomplishment against the schedule plan?

1044. Are significant decision points, constraints, and interfaces identified as key milestones?

1045. How are variances affected by multiple material and labor categories?

1046. Are data elements reconcilable between internal summary reports and reports forwarded to the stakeholders?

1047. Why are standard cost systems used?

4.3 Earned Value Status: Integrated Architecture Framework

1048. Where is evidence-based earned value in your organization reported?

1049. If earned value management (EVM) is so good in determining the true status of a Integrated Architecture Framework project and Integrated Architecture Framework project its completion, why is it that hardly any one uses it in information systems related Integrated Architecture Framework projects?

1050. When is it going to finish?

1051. Earned value can be used in almost any Integrated Architecture Framework project situation and in almost any Integrated Architecture Framework project environment. it may be used on large Integrated Architecture Framework projects, medium sized Integrated Architecture Framework projects, tiny Integrated Architecture Framework projects (in cut-down form), complex and simple Integrated Architecture Framework projects and in any market sector. some people, of course, know all about earned value, they have used it for years - but perhaps not as effectively as they could have?

1052. Where are your problem areas?

1053. What is the unit of forecast value?

1054. How much is it going to cost by the finish?

1055. Verification is a process of ensuring that the developed system satisfies the stakeholders agreements and specifications; Are you building the product right? What do you verify?

1056. How does this compare with other Integrated Architecture Framework projects?

1057. Are you hitting your Integrated Architecture Framework projects targets?

1058. Validation is a process of ensuring that the developed system will actually achieve the stakeholders desired outcomes; Are you building the right product? What do you validate?

4.4 Risk Audit: Integrated Architecture Framework

1059. What are the strategic implications with clients when auditors focus audit resources based on business-level risks?

1060. What can you do to manage outcomes?

1061. What is the implication of budget constraint on this process?

1062. Does your auditor understand your business?

1063. What effect would a better risk management program have had?

1064. Is there a screening process that will ensure all participants have the fitness and skills required to safely participate?

1065. Has risk management been considered when planning an event?

1066. Does your organization have or has considered the need for insurance covers: public liability, professional indemnity and directors and officers liability?

1067. Are some people working on multiple Integrated Architecture Framework projects?

1068. Are all financial transactions accurately recorded

(receipted, banked)?

1069. Does the customer understand the process?

1070. Is there a clear procedure for reporting accidents/injuries?

1071. Are there any forms the staff is required to sign?

1072. What responsibilities for quality, errors, and outcomes have been delegated to staff (or others) without adequate oversight?

1073. What resources are needed to achieve program results?

1074. Mitigation -how can you avoid the risk?

1075. Is Integrated Architecture Framework project scope stable?

1076. How do you prioritize risks?

1077. Are you aware of the industry standards that apply to your operations?

4.5 Contractor Status Report: Integrated Architecture Framework

1078. If applicable; describe your standard schedule for new software version releases. Are new software version releases included in the standard maintenance plan?

1079. What are the minimum and optimal bandwidth requirements for the proposed solution?

1080. What was the budget or estimated cost for your organizations services?

1081. Who can list a Integrated Architecture Framework project as organization experience, your organization or a previous employee of your organization?

1082. What was the final actual cost?

1083. What is the average response time for answering a support call?

1084. How does the proposed individual meet each requirement?

1085. What process manages the contracts?

1086. Describe how often regular updates are made to the proposed solution. Are corresponding regular updates included in the standard maintenance plan?

1087. What was the overall budget or estimated cost?

1088. How is risk transferred?

1089. Are there contractual transfer concerns?

1090. How long have you been using the services?

1091. What was the actual budget or estimated cost for your organizations services?

4.6 Formal Acceptance: Integrated Architecture Framework

1092. Do you perform formal acceptance or burn-in tests?

1093. Did the Integrated Architecture Framework project manager and team act in a professional and ethical manner?

1094. What was done right?

1095. What can you do better next time?

1096. How does your team plan to obtain formal acceptance on your Integrated Architecture Framework project?

1097. What lessons were learned about your Integrated Architecture Framework project management methodology?

1098. How well did the team follow the methodology?

1099. Who would use it?

1100. What is the Acceptance Management Process?

1101. Was the sponsor/customer satisfied?

1102. Was the Integrated Architecture Framework project managed well?

1103. General estimate of the costs and times to complete the Integrated Architecture Framework project?

1104. Who supplies data?

1105. What features, practices, and processes proved to be strengths or weaknesses?

1106. Have all comments been addressed?

1107. Was the Integrated Architecture Framework project work done on time, within budget, and according to specification?

1108. Do you buy-in installation services?

1109. What function(s) does it fill or meet?

1110. Does it do what client said it would?

1111. Was the Integrated Architecture Framework project goal achieved?

5.0 Closing Process Group: Integrated Architecture Framework

1112. What were things that you need to improve?

1113. What is the Integrated Architecture Framework project name and date of completion?

1114. Measurable - are the targets measurable?

1115. Will the Integrated Architecture Framework project deliverable(s) replace a current asset or group of assets?

1116. What was learned?

1117. What is the overall risk of the Integrated Architecture Framework project to your organization?

1118. What is the risk of failure to your organization?

1119. Was the user/client satisfied with the end product?

1120. What is an Encumbrance?

1121. Are there funding or time constraints?

1122. How well did you do?

1123. How dependent is the Integrated Architecture Framework project on other Integrated Architecture Framework projects or work efforts?

1124. How well did the team follow the chosen processes?

1125. What areas were overlooked on this Integrated Architecture Framework project?

1126. What were things that you did very well and want to do the same again on the next Integrated Architecture Framework project?

1127. What areas were overlooked on this Integrated Architecture Framework project?

1128. How well defined and documented were the Integrated Architecture Framework project management processes you chose to use?

1129. Is this a follow-on to a previous Integrated Architecture Framework project?

1130. What were the desired outcomes?

5.1 Procurement Audit: Integrated Architecture Framework

1131. Who are the key suppliers?

1132. Are all checks stored in a secure area?

1133. Is a cash flow chart prepared and used in determining the timing and term of investments?

1134. Are all checks pre-numbered?

1135. Does the department evaluate and benchmark the performance of the procurement function/ unit against other comparable procurement functions/ units?

1136. Are unusual uses of organization funds investigated?

1137. Are requisitions and other purchase requests batched to reduce the number of orders issued?

1138. Is there an approval policy in which the final cost of an order exceeds the amount originally estimated on the requisition or purchase order?

1139. Is a physical inventory taken periodically to verify fixed asset records?

1140. Does the procurement function/unit understand costumer needs, supply markets and suppliers?

1141. Is funding made available for payments under the contract at the appropriate time and in accordance with the relevant national/public financial procedures?

1142. Did the chosen procedure ensure competition and transparency?

1143. Are periodic audits made of disbursement activities?

1144. Have the funding arrangements been agreed where payments take place over several financial periods?

1145. Is there ineffective internal communication in the procurement function/unit?

1146. Are there mechanisms in place to evaluate the performance of the departments suppliers?

1147. Were no charges billed to interested economic operators or the parties to the system?

1148. In case of time and material and labour hour contracts, does surveillance give an adequate and reasonable assurance that the contractor is using efficient methods and effective cost controls?

1149. Where required, did candidates give evidence of complying with required environmental management standards?

1150. Has guidelines been set up for how the procurement function/unit should carry out its procurements?

5.2 Contract Close-Out: Integrated Architecture Framework

1151. How does it work?

1152. Have all contracts been closed?

1153. What happens to the recipient of services?

1154. Are the signers the authorized officials?

1155. Parties: who is involved?

1156. Change in attitude or behavior?

1157. Change in knowledge?

1158. How is the contracting office notified of the automatic contract close-out?

1159. Parties: Authorized?

1160. Was the contract complete without requiring numerous changes and revisions?

1161. Have all contracts been completed?

1162. What is capture management?

1163. Was the contract type appropriate?

1164. Have all contract records been included in the Integrated Architecture Framework project archives?

1165. Has each contract been audited to verify acceptance and delivery?

1166. Was the contract sufficiently clear so as not to result in numerous disputes and misunderstandings?

1167. Change in circumstances?

1168. Why Outsource?

1169. Have all acceptance criteria been met prior to final payment to contractors?

1170. How/when used ?

5.3 Project or Phase Close-Out: Integrated Architecture Framework

1171. What is this stakeholder expecting?

1172. What information is each stakeholder group interested in?

1173. Who is responsible for award close-out?

1174. In addition to assessing whether the Integrated Architecture Framework project was successful, it is equally critical to analyze why it was or was not fully successful. Are you including this?

1175. Does the lesson educate others to improve performance?

1176. Were risks identified and mitigated?

1177. What is a Risk?

1178. In preparing the Lessons Learned report, should it reflect a consensus viewpoint, or should the report reflect the different individual viewpoints?

1179. What are the mandatory communication needs for each stakeholder?

1180. What are the informational communication needs for each stakeholder?

1181. What is in it for you?

1182. What are the marketing communication needs for each stakeholder?

1183. What were the actual outcomes?

1184. Planned remaining costs?

1185. What could have been improved?

1186. Have business partners been involved extensively, and what data was required for them?

1187. What was the preferred delivery mechanism?

1188. Is the lesson significant, valid, and applicable?

1189. Is there a clear cause and effect between the activity and the lesson learned?

5.4 Lessons Learned: Integrated Architecture Framework

1190. How effective was the support you received during implementation of the product/service?

1191. Were the Integrated Architecture Framework project objectives met (if not, briefly account for what wasnt met)?

1192. How effectively and consistently was sponsorship for the Integrated Architecture Framework project conveyed?

1193. For the next Integrated Architecture Framework project, how could you improve on the way Integrated Architecture Framework project was conducted?

1194. What is the value of the deliverable?

1195. How much time is required for the task?

1196. What other questions should you have asked?

1197. Which estimation issues did you personally have and what was the impact?

1198. How effective was the quality assurance process?

1199. How objective was the collection of data?

1200. Who managed most of the communication within the Integrated Architecture Framework project?

1201. How effective was each Integrated Architecture Framework project Team member in fulfilling his/her role?

1202. Will the information remain current?

1203. How effective was the documentation that you received with the Integrated Architecture Framework project product/service?

1204. Was the Integrated Architecture Framework project significantly delayed/hampered by outside dependencies (outside to the Integrated Architecture Framework project, that is)?

1205. How well defined were the acceptance criteria for Integrated Architecture Framework project deliverables?

1206. Is the lesson based on actual Integrated Architecture Framework project experience rather than on independent research?

1207. How mature are the observations?

Index

Printed in Great Britain
by Amazon